PRAISE FOR THE PORTABLE PEP TALK

"This book is sure to inspire a winning attitude in those who hunger for a quick and purposeful pick-me-up."

LES BROWN, AUTHOR, IT'S NOT OVER UNTIL YOU WIN

"The Portable Pep Talk is just what the doctor ordered. It's that instant prescription you can carry with you to take when you want that much needed lift. Don't leave home without it!"

WALLY AMOS, FOUNDER OF THE FAMOUS AMOS COOKIE COMPANY

"Alexander's book is interesting, informative, but more important, it's thought provoking. It left me thinking about the ways I could change and improve both personally and professionally."

LOU HOLTZ, HEAD FOOTBALL COACH, UNIVERSITY OF SOUTH CAROLINA

"The Portable Pep Talk is a high-energy source of food for the mind. After reading it your mental appetite will be calling out for one more morsel!"

PAT WILLIAMS, SENIOR VICE PRESIDENT, THE ORLANDO MAGIC

THE PORTABLE PEP TALK

Motivational Morsels for Inspiring You to Succeed

ALEXANDER LOCKHART

THE PORTABLE PEP TALK

Motivational Morsels for Inspiring You to Succeed

Editorial supervision by Jonathan R. Lockhart.
Cover and interior design by Brand Navigation, LLC, DeAnna Pierce,
Bill Chiaravalle, and Terra Petersen.
Photo elements by Comstock.

04 05 06 07 08 6 5 4 3 2
ISBN 0-9643035-7-4
Printed in the United States of America

Visit us on the World Wide Web at: http://www.zanderpress.com

Deep inside of you there are powers that, if discovered and used, would allow you to achieve all that you ever dreamed or imagined you could become. This book is dedicated to that you.

Also, I dedicate this book to my family and friends who continuously encourage, love, and support me. Their belief in my passion to bring inspiration and hope to others is the fuel that keeps my flame burning brightly.

Finally, my special thanks go to the men and women whose inspiring and lofty words are the source of the grand thoughts and feelings that permeate the pages which follow.

"I quote others only in order the better to express myself."

MICHEL DE MONTAIGNE

The Pessimist says,
"It can't be done."
The Optimist says,
"It can be done."
The Peptimist says,
"I just did it!"

CONTENTS

CONTENTS

INTRODUCTION

I f you could receive a pep talk first thing each morning that pumped you up with enthusiasm and excitement, how would the rest of the day go for you? Imagine receiving a phone call tomorrow from someone who tells you that a group of your closest friends is going to hold a pep rally in your honor the following day. The big day arrives and as you enter a large convention hall, you are greeted by an enthusiastic, cheering crowd. The band is playing; the cheerleaders are waving banners with your name on them; and everyone is shouting, "Go for it! You can do it! You're the best!"

You are then led to a special seat, and over the next hour you have the opportunity to listen to messages of inspiration presented by the greatest thinkers, philosophers, motivational authors, and educators of all time. Upon hearing these messages, you feel energized with new insight on how to discover and unlock your true potential. Now, how would you feel after attending this pep rally? You would undoubtedly be mentally prepared to tackle almost any challenge or obstacle that comes your way.

After the pep rally, you are told that a personal success coach has been retained to encourage, to motivate, and to assist you in charting a new course for reaching new levels of personal excellence. This coach will be there to support you at any time, to offer continual insight on how to achieve new heights of personal effectiveness, and to help you create a personal growth plan. Your only responsibility is to work diligently at applying the coach's ideas to your everyday life. As you wait with anticipation to be introduced to this personal success coach, you are handed a copy of the book you now hold.

By opening these pages, you will experience your own pep rally given in your honor. I have written *The Portable Pep Talk* for you, to be used as your personal friend and success coach. Inside, you will find a diverse collection of one-minute stories ("motivational morsels"). As you read (consume) each "morsel," you will be given a fresh supply of mental nourishment that will provide all the energy you will need to create a more fulfilling life and to maximize your potential for realizing your dreams and aspirations.

You have the choice to do anything and to be anything: You can change any part of your life for the better and, therefore, live up to your full potential. It is my hope that *The Portable Pep Talk* will help spark a new enthusiasm in you to go out and discover the great opportunities that await you.

Welcome to your pep rally. Sit down and make yourself comfortable. Turn the page and begin an uplifting and spirited journey that will stimulate your thinking, and put a smile on your face and hope in your heart. I'll be cheering for you!

ALEXANDER LOCKHART

CHAPTER 1

THE SPIRIT *of* DOING

YOU CAN START HERE

"What is this place noted for?" asked a traveler of an old-time resident. "Why, mister, this is the starting point for any place in the world. You can start here and go anywhere you want to."

How true! Yet how many of us fail to realize the full richness of living because we always yearn to be somewhere else before starting seriously on our journey to the place we wish to be. Someone should write a book about the lives that have been impoverished spiritually and materially because of the "if" which enters into most decisions we must make—the "if" which prevents us from starting where we are and striking out directly for the goals of our hopes. It is impossible to start from some other place—we must begin where we are, using what we have, and launch out upon our journey.

This is the starting point for anyplace in the world. Look under your own doorsteps to find the material you need. Then, on your mark, get set and go!

LEO BENNETT

ABILITY

Break Free and Astound Yourself

While I was attending a circus which came to my city a few years ago, I was looking for the concession stand and found myself quite by accident in the back where the elephants were getting ready with their trainer to be led out into the spotlight. I could not help but notice that the elephants were standing quietly while tied to a small wooden stake driven into the ground.

I asked the trainer, "Why don't the elephants just pull the stake out of the ground with their mighty force and run away?" The trainer began to explain, "While still young, everyday a huge chain is put around the elephant's leg and then attached to a strong post or immovable stake. At first, the young elephant tries to escape, but no matter how hard it pulls, the chain will not break and the steel stake will remain secure." I then asked, "How can that be? As adults, these elephants have the strength and ability to pull my car down the street!" The trainer explained, "As the elephant grows and has completely given up trying to pull loose, we then remove the chain from the elephant's leg and replace it with a little rope and a three-inch wooden stake in the ground. I can take this elephant anywhere with a small rope and wooden stake and he continues to believe he cannot move and will not be able to pull out that little wooden stake from the ground."

When I finally made it back to my seat with my soft drink in hand, I realized I had learned a valuable lesson that night at the circus. Many of us go through life conditioned to behave like these elephants. Each day we have an imaginary chain tied to us in the form of a piece of rope and stake. We never stretch beyond it or break free from our self-imposed limitations and discover our exciting strengths and special abilities. You have extraordinary talents, skills, and abilities. Discover, develop, and refine them, then break free from believing that you cannot do something great. As Thomas Edison once said, "If we did all the things we were capable of doing, we would literally astound ourselves." Never allow what you cannot do to interfere with what you can do.

There is a wonderful world of bright new possibilities that lies within you, unused. Just as an elephant has tremendous ability to move and lift thousands of pounds, you too, are a *powerhouse* of ability. Once you recognize your own ability you will develop a strong belief in yourself, a belief that could move mountains.

BE A COULD-BE

I'd rather be a "Could-Be" if I couldn't be an "Are."
For a "Could-Be" is a "May-be" with a chance of reaching Par.
I'd rather be a "Has-Been" than a "Might-Have-Been" by far;
For a "Might-Have-Been" has never been.
But a "Has" was once an "Are."

AUTHOR UNKNOWN

IT CAN BE DONE

Somebody said that it couldn't be done,
But he with a chuckle replied
That maybe it couldn't, but he would be one
Who wouldn't say so "till he tried."
So he buckled right in with the trace of a grin
On his face. If he worried, he hid it.
He started to sing as he tackled the thing
That couldn't be done, and he did it.
Somebody scoffed: "Oh, you'll never do that;
At least no one ever has done it."
But he took off his coat and took off his hat
And the first thing he knew he'd begun it.
With the lift of his chin and a bit of a grin,
Without any doubting or quiddit,
He started to sing as he tackled the thing
That couldn't be done, and he did it.
There are thousands to tell you it cannot be done,
There are thousands to prophesy failure;
There are thousands to point out to you, one by one,
The dangers that wait to assail you.
But just buckle right in with a bit of a grin,
Then take off your coat and go to it;
Just start in to sing as you tackle the thing
That cannot be done, and you'll do it.

EDGAR A. GUEST

ACHIEVEMENT

There goes the Neighborhood

Achievers are producers. They don't look back at what they could have done, what they should have done, or what they would have done. They go out and prove that it can be done by doing it. High achieving men and women live up to their potential, making the most of what abilities, talents, skills, and intelligence they do possess. They understand that success doesn't happen overnight, but by taking gradual steps toward the desired objective and then stretching just a little bit further. What is keeping you from achieving all that you can be, have, or do? Often times it's simply laziness. Many times it's the fear of taking risk. The fear of failure and even the fear of success defeats us before we even start. But most of the time you will find that excuses keep us from achieving true greatness.

There is a small town which has four separate neighborhoods. The first neighborhood is where the "Yabuts" live. The people who live there think they know what needs to be done. When told they have an opportunity for something, they say something like, "Ya, but..." The "Yabuts" have an answer. Unfortunately it just happens to be the wrong answer. In the next neighborhood is where the "Gunnados" live. Here the folks really understand what needs to be done, and they would have done it, if they had only followed through. They study everything that is required very carefully, and just as an opportunity drifts past them, they realize what they were "gunnado." If only they would have done what they were "gunnado!" Down the street is the neighborhood known as the "Wishawoodas." These people have an excellent perspective on life—hindsight. They say, "I 'wishawooda' this, or 'wishawooda' that..." They know everything that should have been done, only it's after the fact. The last neighborhood is known as the "Gladidids." Here the folks are a truly special group of people.

The "Wishawoodas" often drive by the "Gladidids'" homes and admire them. The "Gunnados" want to join them, but just cannot quite get around to it. The "Yabuts" could have been "Gladidids," but they're still trying to find the right answers. The "Gladidids" are people that know what needs to be done, and they are disciplined enough to do what they know they should do instead of thinking of excuses for what they wanted to do. One achievement leads to another accomplishment. Believe in your ability to overcome obstacles. Start today and go out and make things happen. Become the best you can possibly be. You'll be "Gladudid!"

LADDER OF ACHIEVEMENT

100% - I did
90% - I will
80% - I can
70% - I think I can
60% - I might
50% - I think I might
40% - What is it?
30% - I wish I could
20% - I don't know how
10% - I can't
0% - I won't

ABC'S TO ACHIEVE YOUR DREAMS

Avoid negative sources, people, places, things and habits.

Believe in yourself.

Consider things from every side.

Don't give up, and don't give in.

Enjoy life today; yesterday is past, and tomorrow is not yet.

Family and friends are hidden treasures. Seek them and enjoy their riches.

Give more than you planned to give.

Hang on to your dreams.

Ignore those who try to discourage you.

Just do it; and do it now!

Keep on trying. No matter how hard it seems, it will get easier.

Love yourself first and most.

Make something happen. Who else will?

Never lie, cheat or steal.

Open your eyes, and see things as they really are.

Practice, practice, practice...

Quitters never win, and winners never quit.

Resolve to reflect on your life experience.

Slow down, pay attention.

Take control of your own destiny.

Understand yourself in order to better understand others.

Visualize your desires first.

Waste not your opportunities.

EXamine your efforts toward your goals.

You are unique of all God's creations. Nothing can replace you.

Zero in on your target and go for it!

ACTION

Never too Late

One day an education counselor at a small community college was interviewing a middle-aged man interested in taking some night classes. During the interview the man remarked, "I wish years ago I had studied medicine. I have always wanted to be a doctor." The counselor replied, "Then that's exactly what you should do. Enroll in some classes on medicine and become a doctor." The man looked at the counselor with a puzzled expression on his face and then said, "I can't do that, it isn't practical. It would take me at least seven years to complete those courses and by then I will be too old." The counselor looked the man square in the eyes, and politely asked him, "And how old will you be in seven years if you don't study medicine and take the courses?"

Many of us spend countless hours dreaming about something we truly want in our lives. We spend our waking days thinking about it. We talk with others about our dreams. We feel convinced that we are fully committed to pursuing our dream. But we fail at ever bringing these dreams into reality because we hesitate to take the first step toward making them come true. We fail to take action. Oliver Wendal Holmes wrote, "The great thing in this world is not so much where we are, but in what direction we are moving." Are you moving in the direction of what you desire in life? Because if you don't know where you are going, you will probably end up someplace else. Aristotle, the great philosopher, was asked one day by a young man in passing,

"How do you get to Mount Olympus?" To which Aristotle promptly replied, "By ensuring that each step you take is in that direction."

Once you have decided upon an objective to strive for, you must take some form of action toward it each day no matter how small the steps may be. The longest journey starts with a single step. Develop a specific course of action and make sure that each step you are taking is leading in the direction of your desire. It is important to formulate a master plan describing in detail how you intend to go about achieving your objective.

Many people fail to take specific action toward the realization of their dreams because they allow excuses to keep them from starting. One frequently heard excuse is, "I can't find the time." When it seems hard to dedicate time toward a specific task it is often because we lack the self-discipline. Time management experts will tell you that you may not feel you can "find" the time but you can always "make" the time.

Many people squander their time being involved in trivial activities inconsistent with their dreams and aspirations. It's hard to take action toward what you really want in life if you are busy watching TV, involved in idle socializing, or just plain goofing off. Reaching your dreams is not quick and easy. It involves self-discipline, time management, and a detailed action plan. Those who exert little effort toward the realization of their dreams cannot hope to achieve anything of any consequence. When you convert ideas into action you are seldom disappointed. It takes the same amount of time to stand idle that it requires to take some form of constructive action. Determine what you want out of life then go into action!

SEE IT THROUGH

When you're up against a trouble,
Meet it squarely, face to face;
Lift your chin and set your shoulders,
Plant your feet and take a brace.
When it's vain to try to dodge it,
Do the best that you can do;
You may fail, but you may conquer,
See it through!

Black may be the clouds about you
And your future may seem grim,
But don't let your nerve desert you;
Keep yourself in fighting trim.
If the worse is bound to happen,
Spite of all that you can do,
Running from it will not save you,
See it through!

Even hope may seem but futile,
When with troubles you're beset,
But remember you are facing
Just what others like you have met.
You may fail, but fall still fighting;
Don't give up, whatever you do;
Eyes front, head high to the finish.
See it through!

Edgar A. Guest

THINK-BELIEVE-DREAM-DARE

Think.

Research, explore, question, contemplate.

Believe.

Believe in yourself with undaunted faith that you "can".

Dream.

Dreams are the forerunners of reality.
Dream big and expect positive results.

Dare.

Have the courage to do. Try. Then try again.
Dream your dreams believing all the while that they
will come true. Base them on the same values and
principles on which you base your life!

WALT DISNEY

AMBITION

Soar with the Eagles

What one great thing would you aspire to do if you knew you could not fail? Why is it that many of us are content with so little? Why not reach out for something big! Many times when we set out to be, have, or do something, we allow external forces to question our ability. More often, it is our own self-limiting beliefs. We all aspire to achieve our dreams but we are often afraid and begin to question our ability to accomplish what may seem impossible. You must begin immediately to create and reinforce your belief in yourself and your dreams by transforming them into a plan of action. Eliminate doubt, despair, and other limitations from your mind. Every high aspiration is an intimation of possible achievement. You are given the power to dream and you are also given the power to make those dreams come true.

One day, quite by accident, a farmer found an eagle's egg lying on the ground. Not knowing it was an eagle's egg, he carried it to his chicken coop and placed it beside some eggs in a hen's nest. The hen, not knowing the difference, covered the egg with her wings and protected it through its incubation period. Soon, the eagle hatched among a brood of domestic chickens. As it grew up it mimicked the actions of the chickens. It learned to cluck, scratch, and bob when it walked. It flapped its wings to fly only a few feet in the air. It ate seeds and insects and had no reason to believe it was not a chicken. One day the little eagle looked up in the sky and saw the most majestic creature it had ever seen soaring in wide circles. "What is that?" the little eagle asked in awe. "That," said a nearby chicken, "is an eagle, the greatest of all birds." "That's what I want to be!" exclaimed the eagle. "You're crazy," exclaimed the domestic hen. "You can't be an eagle. You're a chicken." So, the little eagle hung its head and began scratching the ground. "I guess you're right."

For its whole life the eagle continued living among the chickens, not knowing what kind of potential it had, not knowing it was born to soar. It never tried to fly higher than a few feet or eat different food. He was convinced that anything else was impossible. And, when the eagle died, it died a chicken.

Use your ambition to rise above mediocrity. Dream what you dare to dream, do what you dare to do, and be what you dare to be. You were born to soar higher and higher toward great achievement. Don't allow "*chicken thinking*" to hold you back from pursuing your dreams. You can never soar among the eagles if you continue scratching and thinking like a chicken.

THE SECRET

Robert Collier, in his book *The Secret of the Ages*, says:
"You may have anything you want in life provided that you

1. know exactly what you want
2. want it badly enough
3. confidently expect to attain it
4. persistently determine to obtain it, and
5. are willing to pay the price of its attainment."

WHAT ARE YOU DOING NOW?

It matters not if you lost the fight
and were badly beaten too.
It matters not if you failed outright
in the things you tried to do.
It matters not if you toppled down
from the azure heights of blue,
But what are you doing now????

It matters not if your plans were foiled
and your hopes have fallen through.
It matters not if your chance was spoiled
for the gain almost in view.
It matters not if you missed the goal
though you struggled brave and true
But what are you doing now????

It matters not if your fortune's gone
and your fame has vanished too.
It matters not if a cruel world's score
be directed straight at you.
It matters not if the worst has come
and your dreams have not come true...
But what are you doing now????

R. RHODES STABLEY

DESIRE

Burning Desire

The story is told of Roman general Julius Caesar who was about to send his reluctant soldiers into a battle with the opposition, whose men outnumbered his own. The general knew that in order to ensure the success of his army he had to develop within his men an imperative desire to win. He loaded his soldiers into boats and sailed to the enemy's land. After his troops disembarked on the enemy's shore with their equipment and artillery, the general then gave the order to burn the ships that had carried them.

There on the hostile shore the soldiers watched as the red tongues of fire consumed every ship in which they had crossed. Turning to his men the general said, "You see our ships going up in smoke. With the last means of retreating burned, there is but one thing left for us to do. We cannot leave these shores alive unless we win!" That's exactly what they did. By seeing the burning flames from their ships, knowing there was no means for retreat, the general's men developed a burning desire within themselves that enabled them to advance and to conquer.

What is that one thing you want in life more than anything else? Regardless of what you would like to be, have, or do, you must stimulate within your mind an intense desire for its attainment. You must know exactly what it is you want from life and then transform this wish into an obsession that is unstoppable; one that knows no defeat. Going after your dreams only halfheartedly will if anything, produce only minimal results. When you develop within yourself an intense burning desire and you want something bad enough, nothing will be able to persuade you that it's not possible. Where there is a will, there is always a way. Desire is another word for focused energy. It becomes the inward motivating force that propels us toward achievement in all endeavors.

Countless men and women who are often no more gifted than many others have excelled in a particular field due to their intense desire to succeed. They decided what they really wanted, and they wanted it badly enough to dedicate all of their energies toward reaching their objective. People who manifest this powerful emotion within are driven with a deep determination. They plan, organize, reorganize, and invest the energy needed to accomplish whatever needs to be done. Those who arouse within themselves an unquenchable desire to succeed come to the quick understanding that success waits for those who will never say never. Desire is not to be confused with wishful thinking. It is deciding exactly what you want, believing strongly in your ability to achieve it, and then taking continual action toward attaining it.

If you want something badly enough, you can have it. Not just by wishing for it, but by developing a consuming hunger for what you want with sufficient fervor and then going out and doing something about it. Your desire must be focused and narrowed down to a specific objective, and then you must concentrate all your effort toward achieving it.

Take stock in your abilities. Believe that whatever you want to do, you can do if you want to do it strongly enough. Begin today transforming your desires into accomplishments.

NEVER SAY CAN'T

Can't is the worst word that's written or spoken; doing more harm than slander and lies; on it is many a strong spirit broken, and with it many a good purpose dies. It springs from the lips of the thoughtless each morning and robs us of courage we need through the day. It rings in our ears like a timely-sent warning and laughs when we falter and fall by the way.

Can't is the father of feeble endeavor, the parent of terror and half-hearted work; it weakens the efforts of artisans clever, and makes of the toiler an indolent shirk. It poisons the soul, the person with a vision; it stifles in infancy many a plan; it greets honest toiling with open derision and mocks at the hopes and the dreams of anyone.

Can't is a word none should speak without blushing; to utter it should be a symbol of shame; ambition and courage it daily is crushing; it blights a person's purpose and shortens their aim, despise it with all of your hatred of error; refuse it the lodgement it seeks in your mind; arm against it as a creature of terror, and all that you dream of you some day shall gain.

Can't is the word that is foe to ambition, an enemy ambushed to shatter your will; its prey is forever the person with a mission and bows but to courage and patience and skill. Hate it, with hatred that's deep and undying, for once it is welcomed it can break you; whatever the goal you are seeking, keep trying and answer to this unwanted thought by affirming,

"I CAN!"

Edgar A. Guest

DETERMINATION

Thriving in Determination

There once was a small businessman who had a thriving clothing store. One day his small store was threatened with extinction. A national chain store moved in and acquired all of the properties on his block. The chain wanted his particular location as well, but the small businessman refused to sell. "All right then, we will build around you and put you out of business," the new competitors said. The day came when the small merchant found himself hemmed in with a new department store stretching out on both sides of his little retail shop. The competitor's banners announced, "Grand Opening!" The small businessman determined not to be beaten out by the chain countered with a banner stretching across the entire width of his store. It read, "Main Entrance."

Determination is a willingness never to give up, however difficult the circumstances. It becomes an obsession for winning. It is generated within the person who truly believes that if he or she can only hang on long enough, success and triumph will eventually come. Those who tap the inner power of determination soon possess the stamina and courage to pursue their ambitions despite criticism, ridicule, or unfavorable circumstances. Along with enthusiasm and a burning desire, determination enables us to rise above the occasion. To cultivate the drive and determination within yourself, you must first instill in your mind that you are capable of accomplishing your dreams. Throughout history great philosophers and prophets have agreed on this point: What a man believes he is, *he is*. What a man believes *he can do*, he can do! The French psychotherapist Emile Coue put it this way: "If you persuade yourself that you can do a certain thing (provided it be possible) *you will do it*, however difficult it may be. If, on the contrary, you imagine that you cannot do the simplest thing in the world, it is *impossible* for you to do it, and molehills become, for you, unscalable mountains." When you summon from your heart the will and determination to move forward toward a given desire, then nothing can stop you. With determination discouragement is temporary, obstacles are overcome, and doubt is defeated, yielding to personal victory.

THE ONLY WAY TO WIN

It takes a little courage, and a little self-control
And some grim determination, if you want to reach your goal.
It takes some real striving, and a firm and stern-set chin,
No matter what the battle, if you really want to win.
There's no easy path to glory, there's no rosy road to fame,
Life, however, we may view it, is no simple parlor game.
But its prizes call for fighting, for endurance and for grit,
For a rugged disposition and a "don't-know-when-to-quit."
You must take a blow or give one, you must risk and you must lose;
And expect that in the struggle you will suffer from the bruise.
But you must not wince or falter, if you once begin;
Be strong and face the battle, that's the only way to win.

ANONYMOUS

KEEP GOING

When you're sick and you think, What's the use?
And you're tired, discouraged, afraid;
And you keep asking why they don't remember how hard you try
And forget the mistakes that you have made;
When you're chock full of pain and you're tired of the game,
And you want to get out of it all—
That's the time to begin to stick out your chin
And fight with your back to the wall!

When you've done all you can to carry out your plan
But you can't keep your head up much more;
And the end of the bout leaves you all down and out,
Bleeding, and reeling and sore;
When you've prayed all along for the sound of the gong
To ring for the fight to stop—
Just keep on your feet and smile at defeat;
That's the real way to come up on top!

When you're tired of hard knocks and you're right on the rocks,
And nobody lends you a hand;
When none of your schemes, the best of your dreams,
Turn out in the way you'd planned,
And you've lost all your grit and you're ready to quit
For life's just a failure for you,
Why, start in again and soon you will win
And continue to win through and through.

AUTHOR UNKNOWN

KEEP MOVING FORWARD

When things seem difficult, and life uphill,
Don't look too far ahead, keep plodding on,
And inch by inch, the road will shorten, till
The roughest patches will be past and gone,
And you'll look back surprised and cheered to find
That you have left so many miles behind,
And very soon the tedious climb will stop,
And you will stand triumphant at the top.

AUTHOR UNKNOWN

EFFORT

Cutting Example

One evening a young man came home in disgust after a football practice. He explained to his father that he felt that it wasn't necessary to continue practicing because his team had not lost a game all season. The father took his son to his workshop in the garage and placed a thin wooden board on a work bench and then handed his son a small penknife. He then asked him to take the penknife and scratch a line across the width of the board. After doing so, he locked the board and knife in a cabinet. This performance was repeated every evening after the young man returned home from football practice. Each evening the young man would walk out to the workshop with his father and draw the knife once along the deepening groove.

Then came the night when there was no groove. The last light effort had cut the board in two. The father looked up and said, "You never would have believed this possible with such little effort, would you? But the success or failure of your life depends not so much on how hard you try, but the accumulation of your efforts, and whether you keep at it."

The persistent exercise of a little extra effort is one of the most powerful forces contributing to success. Many times we fall short of our objectives because of the lack of constant and determined effort. People of mediocre ability often achieve outstanding success because they don't know enough to quit. They succeed because they are determined to. They know the importance of continued effort toward their goals. Philosopher James Allen defined it quite accurately: "In all human affairs there are *efforts* and there are *results*, and the strength of the effort is the measure of the result." Every task you perform has an accumulative effect toward the achievement of your long-term goal. Everything counts. The important thing to remember is that you must do something every day, no matter how small, that will lead you toward the final accomplishment of your objective. Small deeds done are better than great deeds planned. You will always get out of things what you put into them. Just like getting interest on your money when you put it in the bank. Each effort that you make toward a desired task will at the end always pay you interest in the form of achievement.

Many people, despite sincere intentions, lofty aspirations, and a knowledge of how to achieve what they want, fall short of true accomplishment because of their unwillingness to put forth constant, never-ending effort. Thomas Edison emphasized this when he said, "I never did anything worthwhile by accident, nor did any of my inventions come by accident; they came by constant effort and hard work." Your success and progress multiplies itself out of all proportion to the amount of effort you put forth. Rising to the top can always be reached by topping yesterday's effort.

As you reach for the highest level of effectiveness in your personal and professional life, always keep this thought in mind: It is usually possible to improve a little more by putting in a little extra effort. It's that "*little bit more*" that makes the difference.

THE MAN WHO IS DOING HIS BEST

No matter how little he's getting,
No matter how little he's got,
If he wears a grin, and is trying to win,
He is doing a mighty lot!
No matter how humble his job is
If he's striving to reach the crest,
The world has a prize for the fellow who tries—
The man who is doing his best!
Today he may be at the bottom
Of the ladder to wealth or fame;
On the lowest rung, where he's bravely clung,
In spite of the hard knocks game!
And slowly he's gaining a foothold,
His eyes on the uppermost roun';
It's a hard old climb, but he knows in time
He will "land" — and be looking down!
The fellow who never surrenders,
And is taking things as they come;
Who never says "quit," and exhibits grit,
When the whole world is looking glum;
The fellow who stays to the finish,
That nothing can hinder or stop,
And who works like sin, is the man who'll win—
And some day he'll land on top!

AUTHOR UNKNOWN

ENCOURAGEMENT

Your the Best

Several years ago in a Paris opera house a famous singer had been contracted to sing. On the night of the concert the house was filled to capacity with a sold-out crowd. Anticipation and excitement were in the air as the house manager took the stage and announced, "Ladies and gentleman, thank you for your enthusiastic support. I am afraid that due to illness, the man whom you've come to hear will not be performing tonight. The good news, however, is that we have found a suitable substitute who we hope will provide you with comparable entertainment."

The crowd groaned in disappointment and failed to hear the announcer mention the stand-in's name. The environment turned from excitement to frustration. The stand-in performer then took the stage and gave the performance everything he had. When he had finished his last note there was nothing but an uncomfortable silence. No one applauded. Suddenly, from the balcony, a little girl stood up from her seat and shouted, "Daddy, I think you were wonderful!" The crowd stood and broke into a thunderous applause.

Everyone of us needs people in our lives who are there on the sidelines cheering us on as we face uncertainty and move forward toward our goals. Encouragement is what motivates us to do our best. It gives us that much needed spark to fuel the fire inside us, which in turn inspires us to keep on doing our best.

It's a great feeling to have people in our lives who care and are willing to stand up and say, "I think you are wonderful." Consider the words of Emerson who wrote, "Our chief want in life is someone who shall make us do what we can." One of the most rewarding experiences you can ever have is to be that "something" for someone; to be the catalyst that lifts the spirit and brings out the best in someone you know. Encouragement is the one thing that helps bring out the best in people. No matter what your circumstances are, you should always try to provide those around you with this precious, uplifting boost of morale. Be genuinely interested in what someone is trying to accomplish. Speak encouraging words to them, and most importantly, adopt an attitude of positive expectancy toward those you are trying to help. In this way, you can be, in truth, a "best friend".

"There are high spots in all of our lives," wrote George Matthew Adams, "and most of them have come about through encouragement from someone else. Encouragement is oxygen for the soul." There is no happiness quite comparable to the happiness you can earn by giving the gift of encouragement. Giving others a mental lift by showing appreciation and praise is also the best way to lift your own spirits. Can you remember how you felt after you gave encouragement to someone else? Each of us hungers for praise and applause and you should never miss the opportunity to encourage others to make the best possible use of their potential abilities.

Appreciation is thanking, recognition is seeing, and encouragement is the applause that will continue to ring in the ear of those attempting to excel.

ENCOURAGEMENT

It takes so little to make us sad,
Just a slighting word or a doubting sneer,
Just a scornful smile on some lips held dear;
And our footsteps lag, though the goal seemed near,
And we lose the courage and hope we had—
So little it takes to make us sad.

It takes so little to make us glad,
Just a cheering clasp of a friendly hand,
Just a word from one who can understand;
And we finish the task we long had planned,
And we lose the doubt and the fear we had—
So little it takes to make us glad.

IDA G. MORRIS

ENTHUSIASM

Jumping with Enthusiasm

One day an army general was visiting a military base where paratroopers were training on jumping out of airplanes. During a conversation, the general asked this question to a group getting ready to go up in the air: "How do you like jumping out of planes?" The first paratrooper responded, "I love it, sir." He then asked the next. "It's a fantastic experience, sir!" exclaimed the soldier. "I couldn't imagine not doing it." "How do you like it?" he asked the third. "I'm scared to death, sir, and don't much like it," he honestly replied. "Then why do you do it?" the general queried. "This group has a passion for jumping, sir, they're excited about it, and I like being around people who enjoy what they do!"

Enthusiasm is like a magnet that draws people to you. It's infectious, and people enjoy being around it. Enthusiasm is getting excited about what you are doing so others can get excited about doing it with you. As the old adage states: "Enthusiasm is caught, not taught." In the words of Ralph Waldo Emerson, "Nothing great is ever achieved without enthusiasm."

Many of us never come to realize the tremendous power behind enthusiasm. It reflects confidence, spreads good cheer, raises morale and helps inspire those around us. You can never lift anyone to an emotional state higher than your own. Generating enthusiasm within yourself is an important first step toward success. Your enthusiastic approach to life will always be felt by those with whom you come in contact with. Everyone is attracted to the magnetism of enthusiasm. Suppose, for example, that your enthusiasm encouraged and motivated two individuals one day and then both of them were so inspired through this enthusiasm that they encouraged two others the next day. If this process continued, two individuals fired up with enthusiasm inspiring two others, then in a week, one-hundred twenty people would be influenced. And, if people would continue spreading their enthusiasm, sixteen thousand people would be exposed to this experience by the end of fourteen days, and at the end of three weeks, two million people would be inspired with enthusiasm.

Contagious enthusiasm is a powerful tool that can positively impact the lives of others when it is transmitted through your mood, actions, and performance. How do you harness the power of enthusiasm within yourself? Simply by being engaged in activities that generate excitement. Enthusiasm lies within each one of us waiting to be turned on and used. Once you focus your energy on a pre-established, worthwhile goal, your enthusiasm begins to surface as you more forward toward its attainment. Enthusiasm is the outward reflection of a deep emotion that inspires and arouses you to action. Andrew Carnegie stated, "Enthusiasm is a great leavening force in the mental world, for it gives power to your purpose. It helps free your mind of negative influences and brings you peace of mind. Lastly, it inspires personal initiative, both in thought and physical action."

It is very difficult for anyone to do their best without feeling and displaying enthusiasm. To become enthusiastic—act enthusiastic! Let your enthusiasm become the light that illuminates your path to achievement. Allow it to shine on the paths of others.

ENTHUSIASM!

That certain something that makes us great, that pulls us out of the mediocre and commonplace, that builds into us power. It glows and shines, it lights up our faces.

Enthusiasm—the keynote that makes us sing and makes others sing with us.

Enthusiasm—the maker of friends, the maker of smiles, the producer of confidence. It cries to the world, "I've got what it takes." It tells everyone that our job is a swell job, that our work suits us fine, the goods you have are the best.

Enthusiasm—the inspiration that makes us "Wake Up and Live." It puts spring in our step, spring in our hearts, a twinkle in our eyes and gives us confidence in ourselves and our fellow man.

Enthusiasm—is reason gone mad to achieve a definite, rational objective.

Enthusiasm—it changes an uninspired worker into a producer, a pessimist to an optimist, a loafer to a go-getter. Enthusiasm — is the vibrant thrill in your voice that sways the wills of others into harmony with your own.

Enthusiasm—if you have it, you should thank God for it. If you don't have it, you should get down on your knees and pray for it.

AUTHOR UNKNOWN

THINK RIGHT

Think smiles, and smiles shall be;
Think doubt, and hope will flee;
Think love, and love will grow;
Think hate, and hate you'll know.
Think good, and good is here;
Think vice—its jaws appear!
Think joy, and joy never ends;
Think gloom, and dusk descends.
Think faith, and strength's at hand;
Think ill—it stalks the land.
Think peace, sublime and sweet,
And you that peace will meet;
Think fear, with brooding mind,
And failure's close behind.
Think this: "I'm going to win."
Think not on what has been,
Think victory; think "I can!"
Then you're a winning man!

DAVID V. BUSH

MOTIVATION

Jump In!

A wealthy businessman hosted a spectacular party in which he had filled his swimming pool with sharks, barracuda, and other assorted dangerous fish. He then announced to his guests that he would like to challenge any one of them to try swimming across the pool, and he would offer a first prize of either a new home in the mountains, a trip around the world, or the position as president in his company. No sooner had he made the announcement there was a large splash in the water and a man swam rapidly across the infested waters and leaped out on the other side. The millionaire approached the dripping man and said, "That was a stunning performance. What prize do you want?" The swimmer caught his breath and then replied, "Right now I really don't care about the prize. I just want to find out who the person was that pushed me in!"

Many times when we feel discouraged we need a little *push* to get us moving. We often depend on exterior motivators to get us started. But the *push*, in order to have a lasting effect, must generate from within. If you want to be successful each day of your life, then you must be motivated from within yourself.

Self-motivation gives you the power to push forward in your endeavors and break through the walls of adversity. It is the fuel and driving force which propels you in a forward motion toward your goals. Motivation is what gets us going and keeps us trying.

The word motivation is defined as, "to provide with a motive." Motive can be defined as, "something (as in a need or desire) that incites a person to act; moving to action." Every action that you take can usually be traced back to some definite motive or combination of motives. No action can be taken without first being motivated to do so. The feeling of motivation comes from knowing where you want to go and having the will and perseverance to get there. Once you clearly define an objective, you must develop deep inside of yourself a strong, unrelenting desire for its attainment. You must magnify an intense determination within yourself and develop the self-confidence that will direct your actions toward the realization of your desires.

For self-motivation to be effective you must internalize your desire through visualization and affirmation techniques. Effective visualization is a vivid mental picture of you having already achieved your goal. The reason this technique is so powerful is this: Your unconscious mind cannot tell the difference between a perceived event, feeling, or thought that is real and one that is imagined. As you project this mental image in your mind, your unconscious mind then brings forth the desire and actions that will be in harmony with that mental picture. If you can effectively visualize yourself already reaching a goal you will then generate the determination and motivation to move forward toward the reality of achievement.

Start today and turn your motivation into '*wantivation*' to excel in every area of your life. As the philosopher Socrates once reminded us, "A man who would move the world must first move himself."

KEEP YOUR MOTIVATION

It's the steady, constant driving
To the goal for which you're striving,
Not the speed with which you travel,
That will make your victory sure.

It's the everlasting gaining,
Without whimper or complaining
At the burdens you are bearing,
Or the woes you must endure.

It's the holding to a purpose
And never giving in;
It's the cutting down the distance
By the little that you win;

It's the iron will to do it
And the steady sticking to it;
So whatever your task, go to it!
Keep your motivation and plug along!

AUTHOR UNKNOWN

CODE OF PERSISTENCE

Affirm to Yourself

I will never give up so long as I know I am right.

I will believe that all things will work out for me if I hang on until the end.

I will be courageous and undismayed in the face of odds.

I will not permit anyone to intimidate me or deter me from my goals.

I will fight to overcome all physical handicaps and setbacks.

I will try again and again and yet again to accomplish what I desire.

I will take new faith and resolution from the knowledge that all successful men and women have had to fight defeat and adversity.

I will never surrender to discouragement or despair no matter what seeming obstacles may confront me.

H. Sherman

PERSEVERANCE

Keep on Digging

B ack during the days of the California gold rush two brothers sold everything they had and moved west to prospect for gold. As luck would have it, inside a small fault in the ground, they discovered a vein of the shining, valuable ore. So they staked a claim, and proceeded to get the gold ore out of the mine.

Things were going fine at first, but then a strange thing happened. The vein which had been producing gold ore for them ended. They gave up in disgust and decided that they had come to the end of the rainbow, and that their pot of gold was no longer there. The brothers sold their equipment and claim rights for a few hundred dollars, and took the train back home. The man who bought the claim hired an engineer to examine the earth near where the brothers had been mining. The engineer advised him to continue digging in the same spot where the former owners had left off. And there, just three feet deeper, the new owner struck gold. Just a little more persistence and the two brothers would have been millionaires themselves.

Perseverance is your gold mine to success. It is trying and then, trying again and again. It is the staying power that enables you to hang in there when the odds seem stacked against you. A common reason that many people often fail in attaining their goals is that they give up too soon when confronted with obstacles. They will try something for a while and when it appears that the results are taking too much time, they will quit and go look for something that they think will be easier. The difference between the ordinary and the extraordinary is taking that one more step. Take for instance a stonecutter banging away at a stone with his hammer and wedge. He strikes the stone again and again and again, for over one hundred times. Then on the hundred and first strike, the stone cracks. What did it? The hundred and first strike did not crack the stone itself; it was the cumulative effect of the hundred try's before the one that brought results. You don't always get what you want immediately. You have to keep chipping away and chipping away until you win through.

Many times we stop pursuing a goal or desire right before we would have succeeded. Before pursuing your goals, make the decision that you will keep chipping away at your desire until it becomes a reality. Take Winston Churchill's success motto for your own: 'Never give up, never, never give up'. Don't mistake stubbornness for persistence. There are times that stopping and reevaluating the situation may be necessary. You may need to try a different approach. But your ability to 'keep-on-keeping-on' is what it takes to overcome that which seems to be the most difficult of obstacles. The longer you persist at achieving your desire, the more confident and determined you will become.

Perseverance sometimes means doing today the things that others won't do, so you will have tomorrow the things that others won't have. With ordinary talent and extraordinary perseverance, most everything is attainable. When the going gets tough remember the tough get going! When you feel like giving up, push yourself a little harder, a little further, and you soon will reach your own *pot of gold*.

STICK IT OUT!

When your world's about to fall,
And your back's against the wall,
When you're facing wild retreat and utter rout;
When it seems that naught can stop it,
All your pleas and plans can't prop it
Get a grip upon yourself and—stick it out!
Any craven fool can quit,
But the ones with pluck and grit,
Will hold until the very final shout;
In the snarling teeth of sorrow
They will laugh and say "Tomorrow
The luck will change—I guess I'll stick it out."
The luck does change; you know it;
All the records prove and show it,
And the ones who win are ones who strangle doubt,
Who hesitate nor swerve,
Who have grit and guts and nerve,
And whose motto is: Play hard, and stick it out.
And you think you can't last long,
So you, when things go wrong,
That you've got to quit nor wait for the final bout;
Smile, smile at your beholders,
Clench your teeth and square your shoulders and fight!
You'll win if you but **STICK IT OUT!!**

AUTHOR UNKNOWN

There is something that is much more scarce, something rarer than ability.
It is the ability to recognize ability.

ROBERT HALF

It is time for all to stand and cheer for the doer, the achiever—
the one who recognizes the challenge and does something about it.

VINCE LOMBARDI

It doesn't matter how many people say it cannot be done or how many people
have tried it before; it's important to realize that whatever you're doing,
it's your first attempt at it.

WALLY "FAMOUS" AMOS

Aim at the sun, and you may not reach it; but your arrow will fly higher
than if aimed at an object on a level with yourself.

J. HAWES

You do not succeed because you do not know what you want,
but because you don't want it intensely enough.

W. WATTLES

We can learn to soar only in direct proportion to our determination
to rise above doubt and transcend the limitations.

DAVID MCNALLY

Those who try to do something and fail are infinitely better than those
who try to do nothing and succeed at it.

Few things in the world are more powerful than a positive push. A smile.
A word of optimism and hope. A "you can do it" when things are tough.

RICHARD DE VOS

Motivation is an inner drive which grows when you strongly believe it is
possible to change your life for the better.

Persistence is...continuing to work toward the achievement of a goal or the
completion of a task despite seemingly insurmountable obstacles.

CHAPTER 2

GRACE UNDER PRESSURE

KEEP ON KEEPIN' ON

If the day looks kind of gloomy
And your chances kind of slim,
If the situation's puzzling
And the prospect's awful grim,
If perplexities keep pressing
Till hope is nearly gone,
Just bristle up and grit your teeth
And keep on keepin' on.

Fretting never wins a fight
And fuming never pays;
There's no use in brooding
In these pessimistic ways;
Smile just kind of cheerfully
Though hope seems nearly gone,
And bristle up and grit your teeth
And keep on keepin' on.

There isn't any use in growling
And grumbling all the time,
When music's ringing everywhere
And everything's a rhyme.
Just keep on smiling cheerfully
If hope seems nearly gone,
And bristle up and grit your teeth
And keep on keepin' on.

Anonymous

ADVERSITY

Toughened by the Storm

One day a group of people went to tour a furniture manufacturing plant where some of the finest furnishings were made by hand. The tour included a visit to a wood mill next door which is were the wood came from that was used by the craftsman. There a young man watched with curiosity as a worker began to sort through a large pallet of wood. He would take a piece, carefully inspect it, then place the wood into one of two piles. The young man noticed that the larger pile had a sign marked discard which meant that it would not be used for making furniture even though it looked as if it were perfectly fine. The smaller pile of wood was marked good. This puzzled the onlooker.

The young man walked over to the worker pointing to the smaller pile and said, "At this rate it must take you a whole day to find enough wood just to make a chest of drawers. What's wrong with these pieces here in the discard pile?" The worker replied, "These pieces of wood may all look alike to you, but I can recognize that a few of them are quite different. The ones that I have placed in the reject pile are from trees that grew in a valley where they were always protected from the storms. Their grain is rather coarse. They are only good for lumber. The ones that I have chosen to use came from high on the mountains. From the time they were small they were beaten by strong winds, violent rain storms, and exposed to harsh direct sun light. This toughens the trees and gives them a fine grain. I save these pieces for choice work. They are too good to be used for ordinary lumber."

As the saying goes: Rough weather builds strong timber. The same holds true with this statement: Without friction there is no heat. It is when we face the heat from our adversities in life that we are forged into a stronger person. Adversity is never permanent. Only when you allow it to become permanent in your mind is then what determines the impact and ultimate result. Napoleon Hill shared great insight when he stated, "Every adversity has within it the seeds of an equivalent or greater benefit." It may seem hard to find but, in every challenge that may face you, there will always be a solution and many times a positive benefit if you will just crack it open and look in the center.

Adversities and setbacks are continual occurrences and become your steady, everyday testing ground. Depending directly upon the mental attitude you relate to them, they become either your stumbling blocks or your stepping-stones toward success. Just as a gem cannot be polished without friction, your determination and character will be brought to the surface through trial and adversity. Adversity is the grindstone of life. It can grind you down or polish you up depending on your mental attitude.

Adversity should be looked upon as unsolved opportunity. Develop the attitude that every problem has a solution, and a problem once solved is no longer a problem. Minor setbacks toughen and strengthen your ability to cope effectively with the next challenge you may face. Don't look at adversity and temporary defeat as a stop sign. Rather look at them as a sign post that says, stop, go this way instead." Defeat is a state of mind and becomes a reality only when you accept it as such.

ADVERSITY

The tree that never had to fight
For sun and sky and air and light
That stood out on the open plain
And always got its share of rain
Never became a forest king
But lived and died a scrubby thing.

People who never have to toil
To rise above the common soil—
Who never have to win their share—
Of sun and light and sky and air
Never reach the potential they can
But live and die as they began.

For good timber does not grow in ease—
The stronger the wind, the tougher the trees;
The farther the sky, the greater the length;
The more the storm, the more the strength.
By sun and by cold, by rains and snows,
In trees or in people good timber grows.

AUTHOR UNKNOWN

ANGER

Burned Up with Anger

A story is told of the secretary of war under Lincoln, Edwin Stanton, who was well know for a highly volatile temper. The pressures of war made him easily provoked. On one occasion, he approached Lincoln to complain about a certain general. Lincoln advised him to write the man a letter. "Tell him off," Lincoln responded. Stanton, took his advice and promptly wrote a scathing letter in which he directed all his frustration and anger toward the man. He then showed the letter to the President.

"Good," said Lincoln, "First rate. You certainly gave it to him." As Stanton started to leave, Lincoln asked, "What are you going to do with the letter now?" "Mail it, of course," replied Stanton. "Nonsense," Lincoln responded. "You don't want to send that letter. Put it in the stove! That's what I do when I have written a letter while I'm angry. You had a good time writing that letter, now forget about it."

It has been said that if you are patient in one moment of anger, you will escape a hundred days of sorrow. Ralph Waldo Emerson stated, "For every minute you remain angry, you give up sixty seconds of peace of mind." Anger is a powerful emotion. Allowing it to build up inside is like pressure building up in a pot of boiling water with the lid on. When you have a tendency to become upset it is important to find non-destructive outlets for expressing and releasing your anger. Writing down your frustrations on paper is one way to release tension. Before overreacting and becoming angry toward another person you should stop and ask yourself this question, "What will be gained by saying or doing that?" Many times when we are upset we have the tendency to react first and think later. Impulsively blurting out the first thought that comes to mind can have damaging consequences. By remaining calm you allow your mental energies to be directed toward a rational solution. Be strong enough to control your anger instead of letting anger control you.

Sometimes you may feel perfectly justified by giving a "piece of your mind" or telling someone off. But in the long run you will have feelings of regret. You may think that by releasing your anger toward someone you will feel better, but you are jeopardizing your future relationship with that person. There are more constructive ways other than anger that can communicate to others how you are feeling. Expressing to others how you feel about what they say or do in a calm and collective manner will accomplish far more than through the emotion of anger. When you feel impelled toward anger, follow the advice of Thomas Jefferson as he wrote, "When angry, count ten before you speak; if very angry, count a hundred."

Consider how much more you often suffer from your anger and grief, than from those very things for which you are angry and grieved.

MARCUS ANTONIUS

IT'S HARD

It's hard to keep smiling when troubles are piling
  Their weight on your neck till it's sprained;
It's hard to keep grinning when others are winning
  The prizes for which you have strained.
It's hard to be sunny when all of your money
  Is sunk in a hole in the ground.
But how will it aid you, when woe has waylaid you
  To rumble and grumble and swear?
There's nothing that's healing in kicking the ceiling,
  Or hitting the rungs of your chair.
It's hard to look pleasant when anguish is present,
  And yet it is strictly worthwhile;
Not all of your scowling and fussing and growling
  Can show off your grit like a smile.

AUTHOR UNKNOWN

CHARACTER

The House that Morals Built

A young carpenter had worked for a very successful building contractor for many years. One day, the contractor called the young carpenter into his office and said, "Son, I'm putting you in charge of the next house we build. I want you to order all the materials and oversee the whole job from the ground up."

The young carpenter accepted the assignment with great enthusiasm and excitement. The next day he went out to the building site and studied the blueprints, checked every measurement, and every specification in detail. Suddenly he had a thought. "If I am in charge of this project, why don't I just cut a few corners here and there, order less expensive materials, and put the extra money in my pocket? Who would know the difference?" So the young carpenter followed through on his scheme. He ordered substandard lumber, inexpensive concrete, put in cheap wiring, and basically cut every corner that he could. Yet when he filled out his report, he listed the purchase of much better materials.

When the house was finally finished the contractor came out to the site to see it. "Young man," said the contractor, "you have done a magnificent job! You have been such a good and faithful carpenter all these years that I have decided to show my gratitude by giving you this wonderful house you have built as a gift!"

Character is like the foundation of a house; it can be found below the surface. As R.C. Samsel stated, "Character is the foundation stone upon which one must build to win respect. Just as no worthy building can be erected on a weak foundation, so no lasting reputation worthy of respect can be built on a weak character. Without character, all effort to attain dignity is superficial, and the results are sure to be disappointing."

People of strong character will always do what they say they will do, when they say they will do it. They are dependable and truthful when it comes to keeping a commitment. It has been said that, "You may fool all the people some of the time; you can even fool some of the people all the time; but you can't fool all of the people all the time." You may be able to fool others about the kind of person you are for a short time, but eventually they will see through the falsehood and recognize you for what you really are. People will generally accept you for what you say until your actions prove otherwise.

We are all builders of a sort. Some build houses, computers, cars, products of every sort, but one thing we all build whether we are aware of it or not is character. Laying the foundation of good character means never taking ethical shortcuts but doing the right thing because it's the right thing to do. You can never maintain the integrity of your character through deceit and dishonesty. The true test of a person's character is in what they would do if they knew that no one would ever know.

Every day what you think, say, and do will add to or subtract from your character. Develop honesty, truthfulness, respect, and dependability within yourself and you will never have to worry about your reputation nor jeopardize your character.

REPUTATION AND CHARACTER

The circumstances amid which you live determine your reputation.
The truth you believe determines your **character**.
Reputation is what you are supposed to be, **character** is what you are.
Reputation is the photograph, character is the face.
Reputation comes over one from without, **character** grows up from within.
Reputation is what you have when you come to a new community,
  character is what you have when you go away.
Your reputation is learned in an hour, your **character** may not come to light
  for a year.
Reputation is made in a moment, **character** is built in a lifetime.
Reputation grows like a mushroom, **character** grows like the oak.
A single newspaper report gives you your reputation, a life of toil gives
  you your **character**.
Reputation makes you rich or makes you poor, **character** makes you happy
  or makes you miserable.
Reputation is what others say about you after your gone, **character** is what
  the angels say about you before the throne of God.

WILLIAM H. DAVIS

COURAGE

Climbing with Courage

Courage, contrary to popular belief, is not the absence of fear, but the heart to act in spite of fear. It is doing what you're afraid to do, taking risks, and growing bigger through strength and confidence when the odds look like they may be against you. Courage enables you to accept opposition, and then guides you with determination to conquer it. By discovering specific fears that are inhibiting the growth of your full potential, you can then develop the courage to manage these fears and direct your choices in life with decisions which enhance your well-being.

Sometimes before we begin to reach high and climb toward our dreams we often look back at a time when we may have experienced a setback and fallen backward. It then becomes hard for us to bring forth the courage to continue. As you encounter challenges in your life, they may seem as hard to overcome as climbing a mountain, but if you persist, you will learn and grow from them and develop the courage to continue forward.

Once, a team of mountain climbers set out on a expedition to try to conquer Mount Everest. The first attempt failed, as did the second. Then, on their third attempt, despite careful planning and extensive safety precautions, disaster struck. An avalanche hit, and most of the team was injured. A few weeks later, a group held a glorious banquet to salute the team for their great act of courage and their attempts at greatness. As the leader of the failed expedition stood to address the group, he walked over to face a huge picture of Mount Everest which hung like a silent, unconquerable giant behind the banquet table. He then made a fist and pointed to the picture and said, "Mount Everest, you defeated us once; you defeated us twice; you defeated us three times. But Mount Everest, we shall someday defeat you, because you can't get any bigger but *we can*."

Courage is the mastery over fear. It is not allowing fear to take over and control our lives. Courage means persevering when life has dealt you a seemingly losing hand. It is turning your crisis into an opportunity. Each time you are willing to face your fears, you are summoning the courage to rise above disappointments, take risks, and grow stronger. Dare to dream big and awaken the courage within yourself to face adversity and to go forth with your desires. With courage your fears can't get any bigger, but you can!

COURAGE TO RISK

To laugh is to risk appearing the fool.
To weep is to risk appearing sentimental.
To reach out for another is to risk involvement.
To expose feelings is to risk exposing our true self.
To place your ideas, your dreams, before the crowd is to risk loss.
To love is to risk not being loved in return.
To live is to risk dying.
To hope is to risk despair.
To try at all is to risk failure.
But risk we must, because the greatest hazard in life is to risk nothing.
The person who risks nothing, does nothing, has nothing.

THE FIGHTING SPIRIT

I fight a battle every day, against discouragement and fear;
Some foe stands always in my way, the path ahead is never clear!
I must forever be on guard against the doubts that skulk along;
I get ahead by fighting hard, but fighting keeps my spirit strong.

I hear the croakings of Despair, the dark predictions of the weak;
I find myself pursued by Care, no matter what the end I seek;
My victories are small and few, it matters not how hard I strive;
Each day the fight begins anew, but fighting keeps my hopes alive.

My dreams are spoiled by Circumstance, my plans are wrecked by Fate or Luck;
Some hour, perhaps, will bring my chance, but that great hour has never struck;
My progress has been slow and hard, I've had to climb and crawl and swim.
Fighting for every stubborn yard, but I have kept in fighting trim.

I have to fight my doubts away, and be on guard against my fears;
The feeble croaking of Dismay has been familiar through the years;
My dearest plans keep going wrong, events combine to thwart my will.
But fighting keeps my spirit strong, and I am undefeated still!

S. E. KISER

CRITICISM

No Escape

T he story is told of an old man whose grandson rode a donkey while they were traveling from one city to another. The man heard some people say, "Would you look at that old man suffering on his feet while that strong young boy is totally capable of walking." So then the old man rode the donkey while the boy walked. And he heard people say, "Would you look at that, a healthy man making the poor young boy suffer. Can you believe it!" So the man and the boy both rode the donkey, and they heard some people say, "Would you look at those heavy brutes making that poor donkey suffer."

So they both got off and walked, until they heard some people say, "Would you look at the waste— a perfectly good donkey not being used." Finally, they both carried the donkey and they never made it to the other city.

No matter what you do, people may try to criticize your effort. Criticism is pointing out a fault or the forming of judgements. Everyone gets criticized, but it's up to you to learn the difference between constructive and destructive criticism, and to deal with each more effectively. Most of us welcome honest feedback as long as it is constructive and complimentary. But destructive criticism from others can affect our ideals and performance. Often when we receive destructive criticism we allow it to affect our self-esteem and self-confidence, which in turn makes us feel incompetent and inadequate. Remember that when criticism is given it is from that person's viewpoint, and it's only one person's way of looking at a situation. Critics who are negative invite the recipients of the criticism to think negatively about themselves. This type of criticism is counter-productive. Criticism has a valid position only when it is given in a positive and constructive manner.

Learn to be your own person and stand up for yourself and what you believe is the right thing. When someone is trying to be cynical or critical toward you, say something like, "I appreciate and understand how you feel; however, I feel different and here is why...." You alone determine how to react to people who might want to rain on your parade. Eleanor Roosevelt wrote, "No one can make you feel inferior without your consent." Never let the negative criticism from others cause you to give up trying to do that which you have set out to accomplish.

DARE TO ACT

It is not the critic who counts, not the person who points out where the doer of deeds could have done better. The credit belongs to the person who is actually in the arena; whose face is marred by dust and sweat and blood; who strives valiantly; who errs and comes up short again and again; who knows the great enthusiasms, the devotions, and spends himself or herself in a worthy cause; who at best knows in the end the triumph of high achievement; and at worst, at least fails while daring greatly; so that his or her place shall never be with those cold and timid souls who know neither victory nor defeat.

THEODORE ROOSEVELT

TAKE A WALK AROUND YOURSELF

When you're criticizing others and are
finding here and there
A fault or two to speak of, or a weakness
you can tear;
When you're blaming someone's meanness
or accusing one of pelf—
It's time that you went out to take a
walk around yourself.

There's lots of human failures in the
average of us all,
And lots of grave shortcomings in the
short ones and the tall;
But when we think of evils men should
lay upon the selves,
It's time we all went out to take a walk
around ourselves.

We need so often in this life
this balancing set of scales,
Thus seeing how much in us wins and
how much in us fails;
But before you judge another—just to lay
them on the self—
It would be a splendid plan to take a
walk around yourself.

HELEN WELSHIMER

THOMAS A. EDISON'S
ADVISE ON OVERCOMING FAILURE

First, one must have a definite knowledge as to what one wishes to achieve.

One must fix one's mind on that purpose with persistence and begin searching for that which one seeks.

One must keep on searching, no matter how many times one may meet with disappointment.

One must refuse to be influenced by the fact that someone else may have tried the same idea without success.

One must keep oneself sold on the idea that the solution of a problem exists somewhere and that they will find it.

FAILURE

Bright Lights and Big Failures

O ne day a young reporter had the opportunity to interview Thomas Edison at his manufacturing plant. Mr. Edison took the young reporter through the laboratory where he worked on all his experiments and inventions. There the young reporter was able to look at all the ingenious things the inventor had developed. Among other inventions, there was the improved electric battery, the first motion picture camera, an improved telephone transmitter, and the phonograph.

Afterward, the young reporter asked the inventor about the most famous of his inventions, the electric light bulb. "Mr. Edison," the young reporter asked, "I understand that it took you over a year to perfect the electric light, and that it took you over five thousand attempts. How does it feel to have failed five thousand times before discovering a long-lasting filament bulb?" Astonished and perplexed, Edison looked up and replied, "Failed five thousand times? I did not fail five thousand times. I successfully discovered five thousand ways that it did not work."

Through his perseverance, sometimes working up to 115 hours a week, and his concept of seeing failures as stepping-stones instead of as insurmountable obstacles, Thomas Edison became one of the most prolific inventors of all time. He eventually registered more than 1000 patents in his own name and his Edison Electric Light Company, established in 1889, later became the General Electric Company.

One of the most important steps in building your self-confidence is learning to hold your misfortunes and failures in proper perspective. Failure is an event, not a person. Failure and mistakes are the dues you pay to understand the value of your successes. Failure is a natural consequence of trying. If you have never failed at something then you have never tried anything worth failing at. The only time you really fail at something is when you quit trying. As William Arthur Ward stated, "Failure should challenge us to new heights of accomplishment, not pull us to new depths of despair. Failure is delay, but not defeat. It is a temporary detour, not a dead-end street."

Often times the fear of failure becomes a roadblock that holds us back from setting out and attempting something new. We tend to direct our mental energies to what might go wrong, instead of what might go right. Remembering and reliving past failures becomes debilitating to future progress. You should not look backward unless you plan to go that way. Don't let past defeats stop you from moving forward.

When you have made an unsuccessful attempt at reaching a desired goal or objective, view it as the elimination of a solution and therefore maintain the attitude that you are moving closer to a successful solution. Each time you try and fail, you must look upon the setback as a learning experience.

Only those who dare to fail greatly can ever achieve greatly. Many people have had failed attempts and gave up when they were only inches away from success. As J. Paul Getty once said, "If you want to be a success, then double your failure rate. Only then will you double your learning experience to overcome future obstacles and defeats."

WHEN IT LOOKS LIKE I HAVE FAILED

Failure does not mean I'm a failure;
It does mean I have not yet succeeded.
Failure does not mean I have accomplished nothing;
It does mean I have learned something.
Failure does not mean I have been a fool;
It does mean I had enough faith to experiment.
Failure does not mean I've been disgraced;
It does mean I dared to try.
Failure does not mean I don't have it;
It does mean I have to do something in a different way.
Failure does not mean that I am inferior;
It does mean that I am not perfect.
Failure does not mean that I have wasted my life;
It does mean that I have an excuse to start over.
Failure does not mean that I should give up;
It does mean that I must try harder.
Failure does not mean that I will never make it;
It does mean that I need more patience.
The only people who never fail are those who never try.

ANONYMOUS

FEAR

Release Your Brakes

Not long ago, an old oil refinery caught fire. As the fire rapidly burned, the sky quickly filled with a thick black smoke and flames rose hundreds of feet into the air. The heat was so intense that firefighters had to park their trucks a block away and patiently wait for the heat to die down. The fire was quickly raging out of control. Suddenly, out of nowhere, onlookers heard what sounded like screeching brakes as they looked up and saw a fire truck racing past them toward the fire. The truck hit the curb in front of the fire and stopped, and five firefighters jumped out and began battling the blaze.

The firefighters who were parked a block away from the blaze saw this and jumped into their trucks and drove down the block to assist the others. Finally, after a few hours, the fire was under control. One of the bystanders who saw the intense battle that the firefighters had experienced, commented to the news media who were on the scene, "You should have seen it. The guy who was driving that lead fire truck—what an act of bravery!" It was later decided to give a special award to the firefighter who had led the charge and recognize him for his act of bravery.

At the ceremony the mayor of the city said, "Young man, we want to honor you for a heroic act of bravery. You prevented the loss of property and perhaps even life. If there is one thing you could have— just about anything— what would it be?" The young man looked at the mayor and replied, "Mr. mayor, a new set of brakes would be great!"

Mark Twain once wrote, "Do the thing you fear and the death of fear is certain." Fear is an emotional response that stifles a person's true potential and keeps them from accomplishing what they have the ability to do. Too often, fear is all that stands between you and your goals. We are brought into this world with only two fears. The fear of falling and the fear of loud noises. All other fears are learned responses. As Franklin D. Roosevelt said, "The only thing we have to fear is fear itself." Each of us has a built in alarm system that sounds when we feel danger. This fight/flight response is a natural survival mechanism.

Fear becomes counterproductive when our response is unrelated to any real threat. The number one fear that most of us experience is the fear of failure. This type of fear can cause you to unconsciously sabotage your chances for success. We often postpone tackling a difficult objective because we allow our fear and doubts to hold us back from trying something unfamiliar. As the level of fear and doubt rises, so does the degree of insecurity. This causes procrastination and inactivity. It discourages us from setting goals and striving for success.

The fear of failure causes us to go through life applying 'mental brakes' which block and restrict us from tackling a difficult objective or from taking risks. When faced with uncertainty remind yourself that nothing in life is to be feared, it is only to be understood. Put the fear of failure in proper perspective. There is no failure in life, because we learn from all our experiences, and learning is an important part of life. Use your courage and determination to stand up to your fears and face them head-on. Be unafraid of releasing your *mental brakes.*

THE BRIDGE YOU'LL NEVER CROSS

It's what you think that makes the world
Seem dull or bright to you;
Your mind may color all things gray,
Or make them radiant hue.

Be glad today, be true and wise,
Seek gold amid the dross;
Waste neither time nor thought about
The bridge you'll never cross.

There's useful work for you to do
With hand and brain and heart;
There's urgent human service, too,
In which to take your part.

Make every opportunity
A gain and not a loss;
The best is yours so do not fear
The bridge you'll never cross.

If life seems drab and difficult,
Just face it with a will;
You do not have to work alone
Since God is with you still.

Press on with courage toward the goal,
With truth your shield emboss;
Be strong, look up and just ignore
The bridge you'll never cross.

GRENVILLE KLEISER

FRUSTRATION

Locked Out from Opportunity

O ften times when we pursue our goals, we come face to face with an obstacle that sometimes causes us to lose focus on our objective. Continuously putting forth the effort but not receiving the reward of accomplishment, we become frustrated and impatient due to our lack of progress. Usually when you become frustrated you have come very close to your goal but then you hit a roadblock that makes you feel that you could be doing better. Frustration should be used as a gauge to tell you that you are getting closer to your goal but you may need to change your approach and look for new ways to effectively produce the desired result.

Harry Houdini, the great escape artist, issued a challenge wherever he went. He claimed that he could be locked in any jail cell in the country and within a few minutes, set himself free. He always kept his promise, but one time something went wrong. Houdini entered a jail in his street clothes and the heavy, metal doors were shut behind him. He took from his belt a concealed piece of strong, flexible metal. He began immediately to free himself but something seemed to be unusual about this lock. For thirty minutes he worked and got nowhere. An hour passed, and still he had not opened the door. By now he was bathed in sweat and panting in exasperation, but still he could not pick the lock. Finally, after laboring for two hours, Harry Houdini collapsed in frustration and failure against the jail door. But when he fell against the door, it swung open! *It had never been locked at all!* But in his mind it was locked, and his frustration kept him from opening the door and walking out of the jail cell.

What if you had a master key that could unlock anything? A key that could open the doors of success, happiness, wealth, and wisdom. Well, you have such a key in your possession and it is the key of patience. Patience is the opposite of frustration. People who can avoid feelings of aggravation and stress are those who are patient while waiting for the outcome of their efforts. They understand that what is worth wanting is worth working and waiting for.

Everyone experiences different kinds of frustration every day. Life is full of its little annoyances. But when it comes to pursuing your goals, frustration should be looked upon to stimulate you, help you solve a problem, not yield to it. The important factor that allows you to avoid frustration while pursuing your goals and desires is to develop persistent patience. Sometimes this is about the hardest thing in the world to do. Yet patience is a large part of most successes. Someone once said that their secret to success was in waiting. They said, "Often times you've done what you can and you just have to wait. The secret is not to get tired of waiting."

Often we can be very close to our objective but we allow frustration to blur our vision. Remember that it doesn't matter how long it takes you to reach your goals just as long as keep pursing them. Learn to use frustration as a resourceful energy to help you *push* harder on the *door* of opportunity. With patience this door will always unlock and open for you.

GET UP!

I saw an expert skater once, performing on the ice, and wondered how she learned to glide so gracefully and nice. I asked her how she got her skill. She first began to frown, then smiled and said, "Why I got up whenever I fell down."

I knew a note financier, whose riches were untold. I marveled at his mighty nerve in taking chances bold. Once when we were alone, I asked the rich man of the town the secret, and his answer was, "Get up when you fall down."

I heard a famous orator, whose ringing voice brought cheers, and then, in soft and touching tones, evoked a flood of tears. I asked this great man privately how I might win renown, and, like the rest, he told me to get up when I fall down.

"He is a genius," is a phrase you often read and hear. It means, a man who plugs along with nerve to persevere. You may be awkward at the stunt, and act just like a clown, but if you want to win life's race, "Get up when you fall down!"

AUTHOR UNKNOWN

GOSSIP

Better Left Unsaid

In a small village, there was a wise man to whom many people came for advice. One day a young man with a troubled conscience came to him and asked, "I have been telling rumors and slanderous statements about someone which are untrue. What should I do?" The wise man replied, "Fill a bag with feathers and go to every house in the village, and place a feather at each doorstep." The young man did as the wise man suggested. He returned to him and asked, "Is there anything else I should do?" The wise man replied, "Go back and pick up all the feathers." The young man left, returning several hours later. "I could not find any of the feathers," the young man explained. "The wind has blown them all over town." The wise man replied, "So have your slanderous words become impossible to retrieve. They are easily given, but difficult to take back."

Gossip is not always the source of information it is interpreted to be. Once it has traveled down the 'grapevine', it becomes a distortion of information that ultimately hurts the disseminator, recipient, and subject of its contents. Slanderous remarks about someone in the form of gossip or rumors can ruin reputations, poison relationships, and damage careers. Never speak ill of anyone. Speak of others as you would like them to speak of you, with high regard and empathy. If you are ever tempted to reveal something about someone that was told to you by someone else, ask yourself: Is it true? Is it needful? Is it kind?

It has been said that there is so much that is bad in the best of us, and so much that is good in the worst of us; that it doesn't behoove any of us to talk about the rest of us. If you have nothing good to say about someone, then it is always better left unsaid.

If you become the victim of unjustifiable remarks, don't allow it to affect your confidence or self-worth. Most gossip about another person is usually negative in nature, and usually originates from someone who has little self-confidence.

When someone shares gossip with you don't repeat it. Gossip is like a boomerang and by not getting caught up in listening to it or repeating it, you allow it to return to the hands of the sender.

WHO AM I?

I have no respect for justice. I maim without killing. I break hearts and ruin lives. I am cunning and malicious and gather strength with age. The more I am quoted, the more I am believed. I flourish at every level of society. My victims are helpless. They cannot protect themselves against me, for I have no face and no name. To track me down is impossible. The harder you try, the more elusive I become. I am nobody's friend. Once I tarnish a reputation, it is never quite the same. I topple governments and wreck marriages. I ruin careers, and cause sleepless nights, heartaches, and grief. I make innocent people cry into their pillow. I make news and headlines. Now do you know who I am? My name is Gossip.

J. A. CHELEY

I KNOW SOMETHING GOOD ABOUT YOU

Wouldn't this old world be better
If the folks we met would say,
"I know something good about you!"
And then treat us just that way?

Wouldn't it be fine and dandy,
If each handclasp, warm and true,
Carried with it this assurance,
"I know something good about you?"

Wouldn't life be lots more happy,
If the good that's in us all
Were the only thing about us
That folks bothered to recall?

Wouldn't life be lots more happy,
If we praised the good we see?
For there's such a lot of goodness
In the worst of you and me.

Wouldn't it be nice to practice
That fine way of thinking, too;
You know something good about me;
I know something good about you?

ANONYMOUS

GREED

Twice as Much

There once were two small business owners who were bitter rivals and had stores that were directly across the street from each other. They were strong competitors always trying to outdo each other. When one shop owner would have a sale, the other had a bigger sale. When one would put up a new sign, the other made sure that his sign was bigger. They each spent the better part of every day looking out their windows, each keeping an eye on the other's business.

One day, while cleaning out the basement, one of the shop owners found an old antique bottle. He opened it and a stream of dark smoke began to fill the room. As the smoke cleared, there standing in front of him, was a genie. The genie put his arm on the shop owner's shoulder and said, "You have done a great deed and I want to repay you by granting you one wish. You can have anything you ask for, but I want you to know that whatever you get, your competitor across the street will receive twice as much." The shop owner didn't question this and continued to listen.

The genie then asked, "Would you like to have more money? You could be very wealthy, but your neighbor will be twice as rich. Do you want to lead a long and healthy life? This you may have, but your neighbor's life will be longer and healthier. You may have whatever you desire, but whatever is granted to you, your competitor will be granted twice as much." The shop owner thought for a moment, and said, "All right, I know what I want. My request is this: I want to lose half my business."

Greed is often an excessive desire for more than one needs or deserves. It becomes a strong urge or obsession to obtain or possess something, usually in the form of material wealth. Greed is a force that can generate within us a negative competitiveness compelling us to have more than someone else. We try to outdo the other person and feel that they should not get ahead of us. Greed should never be a motivator to accomplish more than someone else. When greed is used to drive your inner desires it manifests itself into a person who is malicious, jealous, selfish, spiteful, and dishonest.

Many times greed can take another form through jealousy and envy. When you experience success you may receive a mixed reaction from others. They may wonder how in the world you did it or they may simply refuse to recognize your achievement. This type of reaction can gradually undermine your confidence and make you feel guilty about your success. The same holds true with envy. A person can only be envious by believing that he or she has less than someone else.

Envy is an enemy of success. Envy and jealousy breed resentment, and resentment can damage a person's self-esteem and confidence. These feelings can also restrict your chances for success and happiness. Greed, envy, and jealousy are self-defeating and extremely negative conditions. As you hold on to these negative emotions, they tighten their grasp on you. Happiness and greed cannot coexist. You must release one in order to experience the other. Let greed be the one you release from your life forever.

HOW TO BE PERFECTLY MISERABLE WITH GREED

Think about yourself always.
Talk about yourself always.
Use "I" as often as possible.
Mirror yourself continually in the opinion of others.
Listen greedily to what people say about you.
Expect to be appreciated.
Be suspicious.
Be jealous and envious.
Be sensitive to slights.
Never forgive a criticism.
Trust no one but yourself.
Insist on consideration and respect.
Demand agreement with your own views on everything.
Sulk if people are not grateful to you for favors shown to them.
Never forget a service you may have rendered.
Be on the lookout for a good time for yourself.
Shirk your duties if you can.
Do as little as possible for others.
Love yourself supremely.
Be selfish.

These steps are guaranteed infallible.

DON'T LET YOURSELF

Worry when you are doing your best.
Hurry when success depends upon accuracy.
Think evil of a friend until you have the facts.
Believe a thing is impossible without trying it.
Waste time on peevish and peeving matters.
Imagine that good intentions are a satisfying excuse.
Harbor bitterness in your soul toward anyone.

LIMITATIONS

Jump Higher!

B ack in the days of vaudeville, the flea circus was very popular entertainment. *(This is a true story)* Fleas were known to be incredible jumpers and the flea trainers observed a strange and predictable habit of fleas while training them. When a flea is put into a glass jar, it will jump out without any problem. The training begins when the lid is put on the jar. The flea continues to jump up and hit the lid, over and over and over again. As the flea continues to jump and hit the lid of the jar, you will notice something very interesting. The fleas continue their jumping, but they no longer jump high enough to hit the jar lid.

The trainer then removes the lid from the jar and even though the flea continues to jump, it will not jump out of the jar. They won't jump out of the jar because they can't. The reason is that the flea has conditioned itself to jump only so high. With this conditioned response, that is as far as it will ever try.

Many of us have conditioned ourselves with self-imposed limitations. We only try so hard because we have an imaginary lid placed over our feelings about what we can achieve. What we believe about ourselves becomes true as we act in a manner consistent with those beliefs. You have extraordinary powers lying deep inside you that you never dreamed of. You are capable of doing things you never thought you could do. There are no limitations except those you hold in your own mind. As the Greek philosopher Plato stated, "The first and best victory is to conquer self; to be conquered by self is of all things, the most shameful and vile." It is up to you to conquer the negative belief that you were not born to achieve and succeed. To reach beyond that which you have ever accomplished, you must first eliminate the can'ts from your vocabulary and replace them with can's. Many times we are quick to sell ourselves short. Like the music teacher who asked a young girl, "Can you play a musical instrument?" The little girl replied, "I don't know, I don't think so, I haven't tried yet."

Often times we accept that we are limited in some way which in turn holds us back by stopping us from even trying. What limits us most from realizing our true potential are the self-limiting beliefs we have allowed to manifest in our mind. Feelings of inferiority, negative beliefs, doubt, and fear hold us back from realizing our true potential. As philosopher Pierre Teilhard de Chardin wrote, "It is our duty as men and women to proceed as though limits to our abilities do not exist. We are collaborators in creation."

Educator Prescott Lecky argues that people fail to succeed because of a failure-oriented self-image, not because of a lack of ability. Negative, preconceived beliefs and expectations build up "mental roadblocks," convincing people in advance that it would be impossible for them, with their "limitations" to succeed.

Admiral Richard Byrd observed that, "Few people during their lifetime come anywhere near exhausting the resources dwelling within them. There are deep wells of strength that are never used."

By turning your self-concept around to focus on your positive qualities, you will soon begin to demonstrate this through your actions and behavior. You will then have the courage, strength, and confidence to 'jump' out and reach great heights of success.

WATCH YOUR CAN'TS AND CAN'S

If you would have some worthwhile plans,
You've got to watch your "can'ts" and "can's."
You can't aim low and then rise high.
You can't succeed if you don't try;
You can't go wrong and come out right;
You can't love sin and walk in light;
You can't throw time and means away
And live sublime from day to day.

You can be great if you'll be good
And do good things like you know you should.
You can ascend life's upward road,
Although you bear a heavy load;
You can be honest, truthful and clean,
By turning from the low and mean;
You can uplift the souls of women and men
By words and deed, or by your pen.

So watch your "can'ts" and watch your "can's."
And watch your walks and watch your stands,
And watch the way you talk and act
And do not take the false for fact;
And watch indeed the way you take,
And watch the things that mar or make;
For life is great to every woman and man
Who lives to do the best they can.

A N O N Y M O U S

87

MISTAKES

Don't Study the Wrong Thing

To march forward and accomplish great things in your life you must first cease dwelling on past mistakes. You are limiting your true potential by thinking about what you may have done poorly. Take stock of your present achievements and successes. Start today by focusing on the positive events in your life. In Lewis Carroll's great classic, *Alice in Wonderland,* Alice and the Mad Hatter have a conversation that helps understand this concept:

Alice: Where I come from, people study what they are not good at in order to be able to do what they are good at.

Mad Hatter: We only go around in circles here in Wonderland, but we always end up where we started. Would you mind explaining yourself?

Alice: Well, grown-ups tell us to find out what we did wrong, and then, never do it again.

Mad Hatter: That's odd! It seems to me that in order to find out about something, you have to study it. And when you study it, you should become better at it. Why should you want to become better at something and then never do it again? But please continue.

Alice: Nobody ever tells us to study the right things we do. We're only supposed to learn from the wrong things. But we are permitted to study the right things other people do. And sometimes we're told to copy them.

Mad Hatter: That's cheating!

Alice: You're quite right, Mr. Hatter. I do live in a topsy-turvy world. It seems like I have to do something wrong first, in order to learn from it what not to do. And then, by not doing what I'm not supposed to do, perhaps I'll be right. But I'd rather be right the first time, wouldn't you?

Mistakes can be valuable if, for no other reason, they teach you what not to do the next time. When you make a mistake you should view it as feedback on how you are doing. Often times we learn far more from our losses than we do from our victories. One of the tragedies of life is that we have a difficult time accepting ourselves as less than perfect. We dread making mistakes, and when we do, we are often too harsh with ourselves. However, avoiding new challenges for fear you might make a mistake could be the biggest mistake of all.

Mistakes give you the opportunity to learn and grow in the process of rising above them. They show you what you're doing that needs improvement. You will always travel down the road of unhappiness if you demand that you be faultless. Do not waste time over past regrets, losses or disappointments but instead look forward to new opportunities. If you make a mistake and fall, pick yourself up, dust yourself off, and start all over again with a new approach. Focus your mind and energy on the work that now lies before you, not on the fear of making a mistake.

The remedy for worry, anxiety, and fear is to have new interests and responsibilities. Take all reasonable measures to avoid repeating past mistakes. If you do make a mistake, don't look for where you fell, but where you may have slipped.

START WHERE YOU STAND

Start where you stand and never mind the past,
The past won't help you in beginning new,
If you have left it all behind at last
Why, that's enough, you're done with it, you're through;
This is another chapter in the book
This is another race that you have planned,
Don't give the vanished days a backward look,
Start where you stand.

The world won't care about your old defeats
If you can start anew and win success,
The future is your time, and time is fleet
And there is much of work and strain and stress;
Forget the buried woes and dead despairs,
Here is a brand new trail right at hand,
The future is for those who do and dare,
Start where you stand.

Old failures will not halt, old triumphs aid,
Today's the thing, tomorrow soon will be;
Get in the fight and face it unafraid,
And leave the past to ancient history;
What has been, has been;
leave yesterday's mistakes unsaid
And by them you are neither blessed nor banned,
Take courage, be brave and drive ahead,
You can began now and start where you stand.

BERTON BRALEY

NEGATIVITY

Stinky Outlook

One Sunday afternoon, a cranky grandfather was visiting his family. After lunch, he decided he would lie down and take a nap. His grandchildren wanted to have a little fun so as a practical joke, they snuck quietly into the bedroom and put Limburger cheese in his mustache. Soon, the grandfather awoke sniffing. "Why this room stinks," he exclaimed as he got up and went out into the kitchen. He wasn't there long until he decided that the kitchen smelled too. Through the house he went, finding every room smelling the same. Desperately he made his way outside for a breath of fresh air. Much to his surprise, the open air brought no relief, and he proclaimed, "The whole world stinks!"

This story illustrates that when you allow your mind to be filled with negativism, you will carry the attitude that the whole world "smells bad." Everything you experience and everyone you encounter will carry the "scent" of your attitude and outlook.

A Greek Philosopher once stated, "Your world is an outer manifestation of your inner thoughts and attitudes. As within, so without." Research has clearly established that negativity leads to increased stress along with mental and physical health problems. It's hard to maintain a positive attitude and outlook when surrounded every day with negativity. For example look at the evening news. News reporting usually focuses on bad events instead of the good ones. Even the weather is often reported as a twenty percent chance for rain, instead of an eighty percent chance for a beautiful sunny day. Newspapers report plane crashes but fail to report on the thousands of planes that reach their destinations safely every day. A large majority of negativity comes from other people, negative thinkers with whom we come in contact with and allow to affect our own attitude and perceptions. The important thing to remember is that your attitude is the one thing over which you have complete control, not anyone else. It then becomes your sole decision whether you will allow a negative circumstance or the negativity from exterior sources change your attitude and outlook.

Everyone has to learn how to manage negativity, whether it's from other sources or generated from within. Many times we allow our own negative thought patterns to undermine our success and happiness. Our mind may be likened to a garden. The thoughts we hold in our mind are the seeds. Whatever we plant will grow in exact kind. In a garden, if you plant potatoes you will harvest potatoes, not turnips. Whatever seeds or thoughts you allow to occupy your mind will likewise grow. If you plant negative thoughts you will get negative results in your life.

Psychology has taught us that destructive thoughts can be forced out of our minds simply by substituting good thoughts. Negative thought patterns hold us back from constructively finding solutions to problems. Negative thinking gives you a gray outlook on life and detours you from accomplishing your goals. Identify and remove the sources of negativity in your life. Cultivate your mental garden by planting positive seeds of thought into your mind each day.

GLOOM OR GLEAM

It's a cheery old world when you're cheerful,
And a glad old world when you're glad.
But whether you play or go toiling away
It's a sad old world when you're sad.

It's a grand old world when you're great
And a mean old world when you're small,
It's a world full of hate for the foolish who prate
On the uselessness of it all.

It's a beautiful world to see,
Or it's dismal in every zone,
The thing it must be in its gloom or its gleam
Depends on yourself alone.

AUTHOR UNKNOWN

OBSTACLES

Fogged from View

A heavy fog blanketed the coast of California one morning. Twenty-one miles to the west, on Catalina Island, a thirty-four-year-old long-distance swimmer waded into the water and began swimming toward California, determined to be the first woman to ever swim the twenty-one mile strait. She had already been the first woman to swim the English Channel in both directions.

The water was numbing cold that morning, but determined, she continued to swim through the icy water. Straining to make out the shore through her swimmer's goggles, she could only see dense fog. More than fifteen hours later, after fighting the elements, the bone-chilling cold of the water began to numb her to the point of exhaustion. She shouted to her trainer and mother in a boat alongside her to be taken out of the water. They urged her not to give up, as they were getting close to shore. All she could see, however, was dense fog.

Frozen to the bone and her spirit defeated, she later learned that she was only a half mile from the coast! She felt as if she had failed. Later she told her trainer, "I'm not excusing myself, but if I could have seen the shore, I know I could have made it," She had been defeated, not by fatigue or even by the cold, but by the fog that had obscured her goal.

The young swimmer's name was Florence Chadwick, and two months later after being defeated by fog, she succeeded by swimming the same channel and became the first woman to do so, beating the men's record by two hours.

When an obstacle rears its ugly head, it's easy to overlook the opportunities hiding behind it. We often allow unseen obstacles to fog our vision as we pursue our goals and dreams. No matter what we set out to accomplish there are always obstacles in the path.

Imagine an airplane for a moment. It changes course a number of times during flight to adjust to the wind currents it encounters. The pilot generally reaches his destination because he makes corrections when confronted with obstacles like wind shear, rain, fog, etc. Seldom does the airplane change its destination. As you navigate toward your goals, trying to reach a final destination, you'll often be confronted with obstacles. This doesn't mean that you stop pursuing your goals. It does mean that you may need to change your course slightly to adjust to the obstacle.

So often people turn back when they encounter the very first obstacle. Obstacles need not be seen as deterrents but may be looked upon as teachers. When pursuing a goal or desire, obstacles should act as a stimulus to your ingenuity and creativity to devise a way over, around, under, or through the obstacle. Difficulties stimulate you to uncover dormant abilities. Every obstacle you overcome leaves you better prepared for possible future setbacks. When confronted with an obstacle we are often forced to call upon reserves of determination and willpower we never knew we had. This in turn boosts our self-confidence and self-esteem. Always keep your mind focused on the rewards that lie on the other side of an obstacle. Create the belief that what you want is worth the temporary setbacks that may have to be handled along the way.

DON'T QUIT

When things go wrong, as they sometimes will,
When the road you're trudging seems all up hill,
When the funds are low and the debts are high,
And you want to smile, but you have to sigh,
When care is pressing you down a bit,
Rest, if you must— but don't you quit.

Life is queer with its twists and turns,
As every one of us sometimes learns,
And many a person turns about
When they might have won had they stuck it out;
Don't give up, though the pace seems slow—
You may succeed with another blow.

Success is failure turned inside out—
The silver tint of the clouds of doubt—
And you never can tell how close your are,
It may be near when it seems afar;
So stick to the fight when you're hardest hit—
It's when things seem worst that *you mustn't quit*!

CLINTON HOWELL

STRUGGLE

Keep Pushing

One day a little boy was outside playing and found a cocoon attached to a leaf that had fallen to the ground. He took the cocoon to his room and placed it in an unused aquarium. As nature began to take its course, a butterfly began its struggle to emerge from the cocoon. But it was a long, hard battle. As the little boy watched it seemed that the struggling insect was stuck, and making almost no progress. Finally, he decided to help the butterfly out of its difficulty.

He took a pair of scissors and snipped off a small portion of the cocoon's restrictive covering to make the opening larger. The butterfly crawled out, but with its stunted wings, that's all it ever did— crawl. The butterfly's struggle to get through the tiny opening was necessary in order to force colorful, life-giving fluids into its wings so that it would be strong enough to fly. Without the struggle the wings never developed. Instead of flying on rainbow wings among the flowers and trees, the butterfly was condemned to spend its brief life crawling.

Life is full of challenge and struggle, sometimes seeming hard and meaningless. But without strife and struggle in our lives we'd never develop our true strengths. No one likes to struggle with misfortunes and difficulties, but with the right attitude, you can look upon them as opportunities to grow. People in control of their lives welcome struggle and resistance, because they understand that these adversities develop strength and character. Ralph Waldo Emerson stated, "Our strength grows out of our weakness." Struggle provides us the resistance necessary to develop the determination and self-confidence to overcome obstacles. If everything you ever attempted was achieved with a minimum of effort, you would never continue to grow beyond where you are today. Just as the butterfly's struggle gives the strength to its wings, your personal struggles are sometimes necessary for you to develop courage and strength. The turning point in the lives of most successful people has come at some moment of crisis. When faced with seemingly insurmountable difficulties you must keep pushing forward. You will then generate within yourself the ability to fly high above failure and defeat.

STAND FIRM

The battle of life is in most cases fought uphill, and to win it without struggle is almost like winning it without honor. If there were no difficulties, there would be no success; if there were nothing to struggle for, there would be nothing to be achieved. Difficulties may intimidate the weak, but they act only as a wholesome stimulus to those of resolution and valor. All experiences of life, indeed, serve to prove that impediments thrown in the way of human advancement may, for the most part, be overcome by steady good conduct, honest zeal, activity, perseverance, and, above all, by a determined resolution to surmount difficulties and to stand up firm and strong against misfortune.

EDMUND BURKE

THE WORLD IS AGAINST ME

"The world is against me," he said with a sigh.
"Somebody stops every scheme that I try.
The world has me down and it's keeping me there;
I don't get a chance. Oh, the world is unfair!
When a fellow is poor then he can't get a show;
The world is determined to keep him down low."

"What of Abe Lincoln?" I asked. "Would you say
That he was much richer than you are today?
He hadn't your chance of making his mark,
And his outlook was often exceedingly dark;
Yet he clung to his purpose with courage most grim
And he got to the top. Was the world against him?"

"What of Ben Franklin? I've often heard it said
That many a time he went hungry to bed.
He started with nothing but courage to climb,
But patiently struggled and waited his time.
He dangled awhile from real poverty's limb,
Yet he got to the top. Was the world against him?"

"I could name you a dozen, yes hundreds, I guess
Of poor boys who've patiently climbed to success;
All boys who were down and who struggled alone,
Who'd have thought themselves rich if your fortune they'd known;
Yet they rose in the world you're quick to condemn,
And I'm asking you now, was the world against them?"

E D G A R   A .   G U E S T

MAKE A PEARL

Most of us can afford to take a lesson from the oyster. The most extraordinary thing about the oyster is this. Irritations get into his shell. He does not like them; he tries to get rid of them. But when he cannot get rid of them he settles down to make one of the most beautiful things in the world. He uses the irritation to do the loveliest thing that an oyster ever has a chance to do. If there are irritations in our lives today, there is only one prescription—make a pearl. It may have to be a pearl of patience, but, anyhow, make a pearl. And it takes faith and love to do it.

HARRY E. FOSDICK

TROUBLES

The Trouble Tree

A carpenter had just finished up a rough first day on the job. A flat tire had made him lose an hour of work, his electric saw quit, and now his ancient pickup refused to start. As he rode home with a friend, he sat in stony silence. On arriving, as he walked toward the front door, he paused briefly at a small tree, touching the tips of the branches with both hands. Then, opening the door, he underwent an amazing transformation. His tanned face was wreathed in smiles and he hugged his two small children and kissed his wife.

Why the transformation? The tree in his yard was his "trouble tree." He knew he couldn't avoid having troubles on the job, but one thing was for sure— troubles didn't belong in the house with his wife and children. So he just hung his troubles on the tree every night when he came home and, in the morning, picked them up again. The funny thing was that when he came out in the morning to collect his troubles, there weren't nearly as many as he remembered hanging up the night before.

Everyone has their share of challenges and misfortune. Those who live a happy and peaceful life do not allow minor frustrations and inconveniences carry over into other areas of their life that are running smoothly. Effective "*trouble shooters*" realize that their trials and setbacks grow larger by nursing them. They avoid worry and think of constructive ways to deal effectively with their challenges. Often they put their troubles aside and watch them lose their strength and soon disappear. They have developed a belief that 'This, too, shall pass.'

It has been said that a small trouble is like a pebble. Hold it to close to your eye and it fills the whole world and puts everything out of focus. Hold it at a proper viewing distance and it can be examined and properly classified. Throw it at your feet and it can be seen in its true setting, just one more tiny bump on the pathway to happiness. As Calvin Coolidge reminded us, "If you see ten troubles coming down the road, you can be sure that nine will run into the ditch before they reach you." Soon you will come to the realization that a large majority of the troubles you anticipate beforehand either never come or are easily endured.

If you do come face to face with problems or setbacks it is important that you put them in proper perspective. Sometimes this means simply to accept them. Upon doing so, positive steps can then be taken to help you cope effectively with the difficulty and if possible, you can learn to use the setback to your advantage. In many cases you can find out what caused the problem and prevent it from happening again.

You can always salvage something positive even out of the worst situation. Consider it a challenge to find the solution and then benefit from it. Dwelling on problems is a negative and unproductive approach. Your happiness or unhappiness depends far more on the way you meet the events of life than on the nature of those events themselves.

So tonight, before you go to bed, picture in your 'mind's eye' your "trouble tree" and grasp the branches of positive expectancy. In the morning, you'll find that the winds of faith came and blew most of what troubles you away.

HOW DID YOU TAKE IT?

Did you tackle the trouble that came your way
with a resolute heart and cheerful?
Or hide your face from the light of day
with a craven soul and fearful?
Oh, a trouble's a ton, or a trouble's an ounce,
or a trouble is what you make it.
But it isn't the fact that you're hurt that counts,
but what counts is how did you take it?
You feel tired and beaten, well, well, what's that?
Come up with a smiling face.
It's nothing against you to fall down flat,
but to lie there, that's disgrace.
The harder you're thrown, the harder you bounce,
be proud of your blackened eye!
It isn't the fact that you're licked that counts,
it's how did you fight, and why?

EDMUND V. COOKE

WORRY

Frozen Stiff

A young man named Jason worked on a train crew as a mechanic. He was healthy, ambitious, and had many friends, but Jason was a notorious worrier. He worried about everything and usually feared the worst. One summer day, the members of the train crew were informed that they could quit an hour early in honor of the foreman's birthday. The crew began packing up their tools and preparing to go home. Accidentally, Jason was left locked in a refrigeration boxcar. Realizing what had happened, he shouted and banged on the door, but no one noticed.

Jason began to worry, thinking to himself, "If I don't get out of here I'll freeze. Gosh, it's starting to get cold in here." He found a rusty screw lying on the floor and began using it to etch words on the wall of the boxcar. He wrote, "It's so cold, my body is getting numb. These may be my last words." The next morning the crew slid open the heavy doors of the boxcar and found Jason lying unconscious on the floor. The crew quickly rushed him to the hospital. Later it was found that every physical sign showed that Jason had suffered from hypothermia. When the crew returned to the site they discovered that the refrigeration unit of the boxcar was inoperative, and the temperature inside indicated fifty-five degrees. Jason's worry and fear had changed his physiology and he had made himself sick through the power of his own thoughts.

Over ninety percent of the things we worry about never come to pass. To recognize the truth in this statement, write out a list of all the things you were worried about six months ago and you will see that many of them were irrelevant or never happened. It has been said that worry is public enemy number one. When we worry it is like sitting in a rocking chair. It gives you something to do, but gets you nowhere.

Worry is the mind's way of exaggerating certain circumstances in our lives to the point that we convince ourselves that things are far worse than they really are. Many people feel that if they worry enough about a situation or challenge that faces them, the worrying will keep it from happening. When you focus your mind on positive, constructive thoughts when faced with adversity, you soon will discover a new approach toward your desired outcome.

By focusing your thinking on the constructive actions you can take toward your problems, you will find that your worries quickly diminish.

THINK OR WORRY?

You can think about your problems or you can worry about them, and there is a vast difference between the two. Worry is thinking that has turned toxic. It is jarring music that goes round and round and never comes to either climax or conclusion. Thinking works its way through problems to conclusions and decisions; worry leaves you in a state of tensely suspended animation. When you worry, you go over the same ground endlessly and come out the same place you started. Thinking makes progress from one place to another; worry remains static. The problem of life is to change worry into thinking and anxiety into creative action.

HAROLD B. WALKER

NOBODY'S FRIEND

I'm old man Worry, and I'm nobody's friend,
Though I'm called in many a home.
When trouble comes, for me they will send,
And it matters not where they roam.
For me they will lie awake many a night,
And I pay them in shattered nerves.
But they hold me and cuddle me tight—
I'm an old man whom many a one serves.

The rich and the poor invite me in,
And I go wherever they ask.
But they should know I hurt like sin,
And unfit them for any task.

I rob them of friends as well as health,
And things that are held most dear.
And it matters not if they have wealth,
They are not happy when I am near.

But there are two smart ones where I can't abide—
They are Faith and Hope, I declare!
Wherever they go I stay outside—
Because there isn't room for me there.

H. J. ANDREWS

WHY WORRY?

There are two things in which you should never worry. First, you should never worry about the things in which you cannot change. If you can't change them, worry is certainly most foolish and useless. Second, you shouldn't worry about the things you can change. If you can change them, then taking action will accomplish far more than wasting your energies in worry. More often than not, worrying about something does more danger than the thing itself. Give worry its rightful place—out of your life.

ANONYMOUS

Show me someone who has done something worthwhile,
and I'll show you someone who has overcome adversity.

LOU HOLTZ

When we mistake the fire of anger for the light of argument, our lamp of logic goes out.

Character is made by many acts; it may be lost by a single one.

You gain strength, courage and confidence by every experience in which
you really stop to look fear in the face. You are able to say to yourself,
"I lived through this horror. I can take the next thing that comes along."
You must do the thing you think you cannot do.

ELEANOR ROOSEVELT

Don't mind criticism. If it is untrue, disregard it. If it is unfair,
keep from irritation. If it is ignorant, smile. If it is justified, learn from it.

You can conquer almost any fear if you will only make up your mind to do so.
For remember, fear doesn't exist anywhere except in the mind.

One of the greatest discoveries, one of the greatest surprises,
is to find out you can do what you were afraid you couldn't do.

The only way to avoid mistakes is to gain experience
and the easiest way to gain experience is to make some mistakes.

Obstacles are put in your way to find out whether you
really wanted a thing or whether you just thought you did.

In this life we will encounter hurts and trials that we will not be able
to change; we are just going to have to allow them to change us.

Welcome every setback with a grin, for you will never understand your possibilities,
nor will you appreciate your probabilities, until you are put to the acid test of some
unpleasant situation. You will never know yourself until you try yourself in trouble.

CHAPTER 3

SELF-IMPROVEMENT: RISING *to* NEW HEIGHTS

YOU'RE THE BEST!

There's nothing to fear—you're as good as the best,
As strong as the mightiest, too.
You can win in every battle or test;
For there's no one just like you.

There's only one *you* in the world today;
So nobody else, you see,
Can do your work in as fine a way;
You're the only *you* there'll be!

So face the world, and all life is yours
To conquer and love and live;
And you'll find the happiness that endures
In just the measure you give:

There's nothing too good for you to possess,
Nor heights where you cannot go;
Your power is more than belief or guess—
It's something you have to *know*.

There's nothing to fear—*you can and you will,*
For you're the invincible *you.*
So set your foot on the highest hill—
There's nothing you cannot do.

ANONYMOUS

ATTITUDE

Traveling Attitude

A young girl and her grandfather were sitting on the porch one warm summer day as a car pulled up to the house and stopped. The driver approached the young girl and her grandfather to ask for directions. After receiving the directions the traveler tells them that he has just left his old town and that he was thinking of moving. "What is this city like?" he asked. "What was it like in the city you just left?" responds the grandfather. "It was a lousy place. The people there were not friendly, the town was full of snobs, and I never once felt I was part of the community." "Well, I guess that's what you'll find folks around here to be also," the grandfather replied. The traveler said good-bye and drove away.

A few hours later, another car stopped in front of the house where the two of them still sat on the porch. The driver, with a big smile on her face, walked briskly up to the front walk and asked for directions. After carefully writing them down, she, too, inquired, "Tell me, what are the folks around here like? I'm thinking of moving here." Once again the grandfather questioned, "What was your old town like?" "Oh, it was a nice place. It was one of the nicest towns you could ask for," the woman answered with a smile. "The people were friendly, caring and made me feel so much at home there." "Well," said the grandfather, "you'll find that the people around here are pretty much the same." The women thanked them and got in her car and drove away. Puzzled, the little girl turned to her grandfather and asked,

"Grandpa, why did you give those two strangers opposite answers to the same question?" The grandfather put his arm around the girl and answered, "Because, my little one, it's a person's attitude toward a community that determines how the people will respond to them."

It has been said that the world is a mirror, and it gives back to us the reflection of our true self. Frown at it, and it in turn will look sourly at you; laugh at it, and with it, and it is a jolly kind companion. All our experiences whether they be good or bad are merely reflections of our own attitudes. Attitudes are emotional responses to situations, people, and ideas.

Your attitude is the way you approach life. It is a mental tone and outward expression of your thoughts and feelings and it will always give back to you what you send out. Samuel Johnson wrote, "He who has so little knowledge of human nature as to seek happiness by changing anything but his own disposition will waste his life in fruitless efforts and multiply the griefs which he proposes to remove." Your attitude is the key determining factor to success and happiness in life. Whether you succeed or fail in life has little to do with your circumstances; it is your mental attitude that makes the difference.

People who have a positive attitude always rise above their circumstances. People with negative attitudes always blame their circumstances. In order to accomplish great things in your life you must develop a winner's attitude. If your attitude is that of positive expectancy and you believe that you can succeed and overcome obstacles and challenges, then you will. On the other hand, if you have an attitude filled with negativity about yourself and what you are capable of achieving then chances are you will experience negative results. Cultivate a positive, winning attitude. You can alter your life simply by altering your attitude.

BEATTITUDES

Be understanding to your enemies.
Be loyal to your friends.
Be strong enough to face the world each day.
Be weak enough to know you cannot do everything alone.
Be generous to those who need help.
Be frugal with what you need yourself.
Be wise enough to know that you do not know everything.
Be foolish enough to believe in miracles.
Be willing to share your joys.
Be willing to share the sorrow of others.
Be a leader when you see a path others have missed.
Be a follower when you are shrouded by the mists of uncertainty.
Be the first to congratulate an opponent who succeeds.
Be the last to criticize a colleague who fails.
Be sure where your next step will fall so that you will not stumble.
Be sure of your final destination, in case you are going the wrong way.
Be loving to those who love you.

BELIEF

"Check" your Beliefs

A young man had been working for a company for many years, and one day, unexpectedly, the company went out of business, leaving him without a job. He had always thought about starting his own business selling handmade crafts. But he had convinced himself that he could not do it. He believed that it probably wouldn't work and that no one would be interested in his crafts. He also didn't want to risk all the money he had been saving.

The young man decided to take a walk in the park to organize his thoughts. As he sat on a park bench, feeding the birds, a nicely dressed older gentleman walked up and sat beside him. In their conversation the young man explained what had happened and of his idea to sell his crafts. He also told the older man that he believed his idea would fail and he didn't want to take the risk.

The old man listened intently, then stood up and said, "In my many years as president of a large bank, I have met a number of people like you. I feel that if you believe that you will succeed and affirm that belief to yourself often, then you will." The young man said, "I don't believe I can, and I am afraid to fail." The old man said, "Son, I can help you." He then reached into his pocket and wrote out a check. Pushing the check into the young man's hand he said, "I am old and do not have many years left to spend the money I have saved. Use this check to start your business and meet me here exactly one year from today and you can pay me back this loan then." The old man shook his hand and walked away.

The young man couldn't believe what had just happened. When he returned home he unfolded the check and to his surprise the check was for ten thousand dollars! At first he wanted to go to the bank and try to cash it, but instead he held on to it knowing that he could draw upon it at anytime. He now had a new feeling of enthusiasm, and started telling himself that, "I can't fail. I have ten thousand dollars! I will not fail!" Over the next eleven months the young man worked hard building his business. It was becoming very successful. He worked day and night just trying to keep up with the orders. He never once had to cash the check.

On the twelfth month, the young man returned to the park, just as he had agreed, to meet the generous man that had given him the loan. At exactly the agreed upon time, the old man approached him and sat down. Just as the young man was getting ready to hand him the uncashed check and tell him about his new success, a lady in a nurse's uniform ran quickly up to the old man and grabbed his arm. She apologized to the young man and said, "I'm so glad that I found him. I hope he hasn't been bothering you. He's always wandering away from the nursing home and going around telling people he's a retired president of some large bank. What an imagination!" She took the old man's arm and led him away.

The young man just sat there, frozen to the bench. All year long he had been working at his new business with passion, knowing that he had a check for ten thousand dollars that he could cash at any time. At least that's what he thought! It suddenly dawned on him that he had made his new business a success based upon his belief in himself and the attitude that he could achieve what he truly desired, if he believed in his mind that he could.

The single most important attitude affecting human performance is belief in oneself. Anything you believe with feeling becomes your reality, turning the mental into the physical. The more intense your belief, the more likely it will be true for you. As William James of Harvard stated, "Belief creates the actual fact." If for instance you absolutely believe you were meant to achieve great success in life, you will develop the attitude that nothing can stop you. You will also develop success habits consistent with what it is you desire, and you will cast aside those habits inconsistent with what you want to achieve with your life. Simply stated, when you believe you are a success, you will soon act like a success, and in turn you will become a success. This is called the "As-If" principle which states that if you want a quality, act as if you already had it. This is not impractical wishful thinking but rather an expectation to rise above and excel beyond your current condition. When you believe in yourself and your abilities you can accomplish what others consider impossible. As Henry Ford said, "Whether you believe you can do a thing or not, you are right."

Unfortunately, many people pass through life selling themselves short. They allow their self-limiting beliefs to restrain from taking risks or trying new things. Try to identify those self-sabotaging beliefs that are holding you back from realizing your true potential. Eliminate the concerns, doubts, fears, and self-imposed limitations from your mind, because once you believe something is true, whether or not it is, you will then act as if it is. Today, turn your beliefs into a blank check, start fresh and then write yourself a fortune in happiness and success.

BELIEVE AND ACHIEVE

If you want a thing bad enough
To go out and fight for it,
Work day and night for it,
Give up your time and your peace and your sleep for it,
If only desire of it makes you never tire of it,
And life seems all empty and useless without it
And all that you scheme and dream is about it,
If gladly you'll sweat for it,
Fret for it, plan for it,
Lose all your terror of the opposition for it,
If you'll simply go after that thing that you want,
With all your capacity,
Strength and sagacity,
Faith, hope and confidence and stern pertinacity,
If neither cold poverty, famished and gaunt,
Nor sickness nor pain
Of body or brain
Can turn you away from the thing that you want,
If dogged and grim you besiege and beset it,
You'll get it!

BERTON BRALEY

COMMUNICATION

In Through the Out Door

A stranger was walking down a residential street and noticed a man struggling with a washing machine at the doorway of his house. When the stranger volunteered to help, the homeowner was overjoyed, and the two men together began to work and struggle with the bulky appliance. After several minutes of fruitless effort the two men stopped and just stared at each other in frustration. They looked as if they were on the verge of total exhaustion. Finally, when they caught their breath, the stranger said to the homeowner, "Well, it looks like we'll never get this washing machine in there!" To which the homeowner replied, "In? I'm trying to move it out of here!"

Often times we hear the expression, "There was a breakdown in communications." Good communication skills is your ability to express your intentions through clear verbal and nonverbal language. Your body language, gestures, facial expressions, and eye contact help you to get your message across effectively and to show that you have a sincere interest in what the other person is trying to say. Experts tell us that as many as seventy percent of our communication efforts are likely to be misunderstood, misinterpreted, mistaken, misconstrued, or missed. One of the most important, but often overlooked qualities of a good communicator, is listening. Research indicates that many of us spend as much as eighty percent of our waking hours in communication. Therefore it is vital for you to improve your communication skills along with your listening skills. Only seven percent of what you communicate to others is in the form of words. Thirty-eight percent comes from your tone of voice, while the other fifty-five percent is represented by your body language.

Many times during a conversation we are so busy thinking about what to say next that we don't understand the true meaning of what the other person is saying. This is because most people speak at the rate of about one-hundred twenty five words per minute, whereas the mind functions at between four-hundred fifty to five-hundred words per minute. This allows our mind to wander and think about other things.

To communicate effectively you must become an effective listener. Listening builds trust, makes the other person feel valued, and shows that you are focusing your attention on the other person and their needs. Author Leo Buscaglia noted: "Most conversations are just alternating monologues. The question is, is there any real listening going on?" Remember, talk and you say what you already know, but listen and you learn something new.

When trying to get your message across effectively, use clear language and learn not to be vague. Think before you speak so that your ideas are not left open for misinterpretation. When speaking to another person project your enthusiasm, energy, positive attitude, and self-esteem and you will find that they in turn will be interested in listening to you.

Look at your communications as depositing a part of yourself in another person. The amount of time you spend communicating makes it imperative that you continually strive to improve your communication skills both verbally and non-verbally.

COULD YOU JUST LISTEN?

When I ask you to listen to me
and you start giving me advice,
you have not done what I asked.

When I ask you to listen to me
and you tell me I shouldn't feel that way,
you are trampling on my feelings.

When I ask you to listen to me
and you try to solve my problems for me,
you have failed me.

Listen! All I asked was that you listen,
not talk to or do—
Just hear me.

I can do for myself; I'm not helpless—
maybe discouraged and faltering,
but not helpless.
So please listen and just hear me.

And if you want to talk,
wait a minute for your turn—
and I'll listen to you.

ANONYMOUS

TEN COMMON SENSE RULES
OF HUMAN RELATIONS

Speak to people. There's nothing as nice as a cheerful greeting.

Smile at people. It takes 112 muscles to frown and only 13 to smile.

Call people by their name. The sweetest music to the ears is one's own name.

Be friendly and helpful. Radiate friendship and it will be returned tenfold.

Be cordial. Speak and act as if everything you did were a pleasure.

Be genuinely interested in people.

Be generous with praise, cautious with criticism.

Be considerate with the feelings of others; it will be appreciated.

Be thoughtful of others opinions. There are three sides to every controversy—yours, the others—and the right one.

Be alert to give service. What counts a great deal in life is what we do for others.

DALE CARNEGIE

CONFIDENCE

What You See is What You Get

There was once a handsome prince who had a crooked back. This limitation kept him from attaining his full potential as the kind of prince he dreamt to be. On his fifteenth birthday the king asked him what he would like to receive as a birthday gift. Bent over and looking up, the boy replied, "I would like a statue of myself."

"Surely there must be something else you desire," the king asked. "No, I want a statue of myself. But I do not want it to be made as I appear now. Rather I would like a statue of how I would look if I stood straight!" So the king commissioned the best sculptor in the land to carve the statue as the young prince requested. When it was finished, the king had it placed in the prince's private garden outside his bedroom window where he could see it every day.

Each morning the young prince would look out at his likeness and study the statue, straining and stretching as best he could to mimic the clay replica. As time went on, people began to say, "Do you notice, the prince's back doesn't seem to be as crooked as it was." The prince overheard these remarks and began to gain more confidence in himself. Then one day a remarkable thing happened. The prince reached high overhead, stretching as far as he could reach, and suddenly found himself standing tall and erect, staring straight at the clay image in the garden.

Much has been written about success and happiness and how you can attain it. The basic premise found in these works is that you must set goals for yourself and then work persistently and positively toward them. This of course is true, but it is impossible to move forward toward their attainment unless you have confidence in yourself and in your abilities. Many men and women richly endowed with ability and talent have failed because they lacked sufficient self-confidence. Others who are not so favored by mother nature have become successful because of their unshakable confidence. The true test of an individual's confidence is what he or she does when faced with a seemingly impossible situation. True confidence lies in the philosophy of "I can" instead of the "I can't." It is the underlying attitude that says, "I've got what it takes." People with supreme confidence learn to stretch beyond their comfort zones and will go on doing the impossible while others are saying it can't be done.

Confidence is a growing spirit of assuredness flowing from the awareness that you are on the right road to achievement. Confidence is a direct result of positive experience. The more positive experiences you gain, the more confidence you will possess. Each day, you should look over your small successes and use them to reinforce your confidence. Many times we don't perceive the little things that we do as anything extraordinary.

By recognizing past achievements, you begin to feel good about yourself and what you are capable of achieving. As you begin to build on this confidence, you stretch and strengthen your mental muscles, giving you the ability to deal effectively with the obstacles and challenges that may confront you as you pursue your goals. Take time to evaluate your positive qualities. You will find that there are many more than you may think.

BELIEVING IN YOURSELF

Doubt can stop you in your tracks
It can drain away desire,
Believing, on the other hand,
Can set your world afire.

When you hold the opinion that
You can reach that special dream,
You have the edge needed to make
Achieving much easier than it may seem.

Believing in your ability
Affects the way you act,
And produces an air of confidence
Which influences how others will react.

When you believe you can achieve
And believe it with all your soul,
You possess a powerful asset
You most likely will reach your goal.

ANONYMOUS

EXCELLENCE

And Then Some!

A young woman was interviewing a successful business man as part of her college thesis. At the end of the interview she asked him if he could share with her his secret to success. After carefully pondering her question, the business man replied, "I can sum it up in three words—*and then some*." "You see," he said, "I have learned that the difference between average people and the truly successful could be simply stated in those three words. Top performers, those who are devoted to excellence, did what was expected—*and then some*." He then continued, "These type of people are thoughtful of others; they are considerate and kind—*and then some*. Top performers meet their obligations and responsibilities fairly and squarely—*and then some*. They are good friends and helpful to their neighbors—*and then some*. They give generously of their time— *and then some*. They greet those they meet with a smile and enthusiasm—*and then some*."

The business man then got up from his chair and escorted the young women to the door. As she thanked him and shook his hand, the executive shared with her his final thought: "Just remember, in any endeavor always go beyond what is expected. Be committed to excellence. Go a little bit further—*and then some*."

It will only be a matter of time until you reach the top in all your endeavors if you can contrive each day to outperform the person you were yesterday. Your true success in life begins only when you make the commitment to becoming excellent at whatever you do.

Without this commitment you will always perform at lower levels than you are capable of and you will never achieve your full potential. A commitment to excellence is the underlying characteristic of a successful person. Anything less is an acceptance of mediocrity. Pursuing excellence in your life means taking steps beyond satisfaction and complacency.

Excellence is your ability to motivate yourself to do what you should do, when you should do it, whether you feel like it or not. It is going the extra mile at work and in every task that you set out to accomplish. It is devoting yourself to constant and never ending improvement in all areas of your life. Striving toward excellence reinforces your self-esteem, improves your self-image, builds your self-confidence, and improves your performance in every other area of your life.

Look at the truly successful people around you and you will see that they have set high standards for themselves. These successful people have learned that just enough to get by is not enough to get ahead. They are willing to go the second mile. They understand that excellent rewards come from excellent performance. Successful men and women strive to give one hundred percent of themselves in everything they do—*and then some.*

EXCELLENCE CAN BE ATTAINED IF YOU...

Care more than others think is wise.
Risk more than others think is safe.
Dream more than others think is practical.
Expect more than others think is possible.

COMMITMENT TO EXCELLENCE

Giving one-hundred percent and striving to do your very best in all areas of your life is committing to excellence. One study shows what would happen if things were done right only 99.9 percent of the time.

One hour of unsafe drinking water every month.

103,260 income tax returns would be processed incorrectly this year.

1,314 phone calls would be misrouted every minute.

107 incorrect medical procedures would be performed by the end of the day today.

880,000 credit cards in circulation would turn out to have incorrect cardholder information on their magnetic strips.

20,000 incorrect drug prescriptions would be written in the next twelve months.

2 unsafe plane landings per day at the nation's busiest airport.

16,000 pieces of mail lost by the U.S. Postal Service every hour.

20,000 incorrect drug prescriptions per year.

500 incorrect surgical operations per week.

50 newborn babies dropped at birth by doctors every day.

22,000 checks deducted from the wrong bank account each hour.

32,000 missed heartbeats per person per year.

Commit yourself to excellence.
Develop an attitude that refuses to accept anything less than your best.

GOALS

Ready! Aim! Goal!

An archery instructor was out in a field with two of her students teaching them the fundamentals of using a bow and arrow. Hanging from a tree in the distance was a small target. The first student took an arrow from his quiver, readied it in his bow, and took aim. The instructor asked him to describe everything he saw. "I see the sky, the clouds, the trees, and leaves, the branches and the target," he answered. "Put your bow down," the instructor said. "You are not ready."

The second student stepped up and readied his bow with an arrow. "Please describe everything you see?" the instructor asked. "There is only the target in sight," answered the second student. "Then shoot!" the instructor commanded. The arrow flew straight ahead and hit the target. "Very good," said the instructor. "When you see only the target, your aim will be true, and your arrows will fly according to your wish."

Consider this: a traveler planning a vacation knows where he is going. A skilled archer sets his sights on a specific target focusing on it until he hits the bull's eye. All of us have heard over and over again the importance of setting goals. Why is it then that so many of us don't implement a goal-setting strategy into our lives? Successful people are always the ones who aim their lives toward a specific objective and then work diligently and persistently to accomplish that which they set out to do. Goals are targets of success. You can never experience the thrill of hitting the bull's eye if you don't know what the target is. Only a small percentage of people, (actually studies show only ten percent) have specific, clear, defined goals. People who are successful and who frequently reach their goals are those who have developed the habit of writing them down, reviewing them often, and having a concise plan on how to reach them. A survey given to a graduation class at Yale University many years ago illustrates the power behind setting goals. One of the questions on the survey was, "Do you have written goals and a strategy for there attainment?" Only three percent responded "yes." Ten years later a follow-up study showed that the three percent who answered "yes" had accomplished more financially and professionally than the remaining ninety-seven percent!

Having clear objectives in life is very important. Because in the absence of a goal to be achieved, you have no standard for judging whether you are getting anywhere. Simply, your life can't go according to plan if you have no plan. Goals are important because they give you a feeling of purpose. Goals are something you can aim your life toward. They are a destination—something to reach for. They give you direction. The challenges involved in reaching a goal bring growth and develop character. When you accomplish your goals you experience the joy of achievement.

One of the major causes of failing to reach a goal is that many people get so concerned about the possible obstacles they are likely to encounter that they give up before they ever start. Begin today and define what it is you want from life. It is essential to know exactly and specifically what you want. Write your desires down on paper. Don't worry about how far the target is. Just keep sight of the bull's eye. Then take aim with desire, focus, and persistence; and fire away!

GO FOR THE GOAL!

Fortunate are the persons,
Who in this life can find
A purpose that can fill their days,
And goals to fill their minds!

The world is filled with many people,
Content with where they are;
Not knowing joys success can bring,
No will to go that far.

Yet in this world there is a need
For people to lead the rest,
To rise above the "average" life,
By giving of their best!

Would you be the one who dares to try
When challenged by the task?
To rise to heights you've never seen,
Or is that too much to ask?

This is your day—a world to win,
Great purpose to achieve
Accept the challenge of your goals
And in yourself believe!

ANONYMOUS

HABIT

Secret of the Touchstone

When the great Library of Alexandria caught fire and burned, an old man found amidst the debris one book. It had been saved by the fire and within the pages it told the secret of the "Touchstone."

The writing went on to explain that the touchstone was a small pebble that could turn any common metal into pure gold and that it could be found on the shores of the Black Sea, lying among thousands of other pebbles which looked exactly like it. But here lay the secret: The real touchstone would feel warm, while ordinary pebbles are cold. So the man sold his few belongings, bought some simple supplies, and camped out on the shoreline and began searching among the pebbles.

He knew that if he picked up ordinary pebbles and threw them down because they were cold, he might pick up the same pebble hundreds of times. So, when he felt one that was cold he threw it into the sea. His hope was fading as he spent weeks, months, and years searching for the touchstone. Yet he continued his routine—pick up a pebble, it's cold, throw it in the sea. He went on and on and on this way. But one morning he picked up a pebble that was warm. And inadvertently he still threw it into the sea! He had gotten so into the habit of throwing them into the sea, that when the one he wanted came along, he still threw it away!

Aristotle once wrote, "You are what you repeatedly do." What you repeatedly do through your thoughts and actions are what become your habits. Habits can either be the worst of your enemies or the best of your servants. As the saying goes, "We're all creatures of habit." Habits are conditioned responses formed through repetition, repeating a particular action until it becomes second nature. Habits are usually unconscious behaviors. Once formed, we don't have to think about them, they are not always easy to change, and most of the time they are so automatic that we're not always aware of the habits we have acquired. Almost everything you do is a result of habit. The way you comb your hair, the way you drive your car, and the way you sign your name, are just a few things that are done out of habit.

Habits are good only so long as they serve you in a way which improves and enriches your life. This means first identifying and then eliminating negative habits which are self-destructive. You must develop the willpower to eliminate in yourself every weak and undesirable habit and then create new behaviors and actions consistent with what you want to be, have, and do in your life. You can change your habits if you really want to. The important thing is to admit that you have a bad habit, make the decision to change it, and then get started. This is essential, for habits, good or bad, grow stronger with time. Shakespeare said it best when he wrote, "First we make our habits, then our habits make us."

Can you think of any bad habits that you currently have that are unconstructive, destructive, and that are working against you? Today, begin developing the habits of a winner. Form the mental habit of thinking and acting confidently, positively, and courageously. Cast aside those behaviors and actions that are causing you both mental and physical discomfort.

CONSTANT COMPANION

I am your constant companion. I am your greatest helper or heaviest burden. I will push you onward or drag you down to failure. I am completely at your command. Half the things you do you might just as well turn over to me and I will be able to do them quickly and correctly. I am easily managed—you must merely be firm with me. Show me exactly how you want something done and after a few lessons I will do it automatically.

I am the servant of all great men; and alas, of all failures. Those who are great, I have made great. Those who are failures, I have made failures. I am not a machine, though I work with all the precision of a machine plus the intelligence of a man. You may run me for profit or run me for ruin—it makes no difference to me.

Take me, train me, be firm with me, and I will place the world at your feet. Be easy with me and I will destroy you. You know who I am. I am a close friend. My name is **HABIT!**

A U T H O R   U N K N O W N

SOUND VALUES

Marshall Field once indicated the following twelve reminders that can be helpful in obtaining a sound sense of values:

The value of time.
The success of perseverance.
The pleasure of working.
The dignity of simplicity.
The worth of character.
The power of kindness.
The influence of example.
The obligation of duty.
The wisdom of economy.
The virtue of patience.
The improvement of talent.
The joy of originating.

HONESTY

Caught Cold Handed

A woman, preparing to entertain dinner guests, went to a small grocery store to buy food. She stopped at the meat counter and asked the attendant for a large chicken. He reached down into the cold storage compartment, grabbed the last chicken he had, and placed it on the scale. "This one weighs four pounds ma'am," he said. "I'm not sure that will be enough," the woman replied. "Don't you have anything bigger?" The attendant took the chicken off the scale and placed it back into the compartment. He then pretended to search through the melting ice for another one, and then brought out the same bird, discreetly applying some finger pressure to the scale. "Ah," he said with a smile, "this one weighs six pounds." "I'm just not sure," the women said with a frown. "I'll tell you what— wrap them up for me, I'll take them both!"

Honesty is one of the most valuable of personal assets. It is not merely honesty of action, but honesty of intention. It is being fair and candid in your dealings with others. The foundation of a successful life is built on honesty; being honest and trustworthy at your job, in your relationships, and in business. It requires far less effort to go through each day as someone who is truthful than someone who is deceitful. Many people have destroyed their lives by dishonest behavior. Honesty is always the best policy and you must realize that you can go far in life with personal integrity and nowhere without it. It has been said that honesty is the one card in the pack that you can play at any time without thinking of how to play it. You can always measure the honesty of a person by how likely they are to do what is right and moral under all conditions—despite any temptation to cut corners or be untruthful. When you practice unscrupulous behavior and conduct, it will always come back to you in the way of reproach or shame. It is like throwing sand against a strong wind. Always practice the golden rule: 'Do unto others as you would have them do unto you.' If you should find yourself involved in any fraudulent or dishonest action ask yourself this question, "What kind of world would this world be if everybody in it was just like me?"

Never jeopardize your honesty and integrity because when you do, you jeopardize your reputation as a person of high qualities and morals. As the old adage says, "When you never shame, you never have to explain." Integrity is the result of self-discipline, inner trust, and a decision to be honest in all situations.

Your success in life does not rest solely upon your mental attributes, but upon your moral qualities. Live each day as if your life were being judged by your intent and actions. Be open, honest, and credible when dealing with others. When you develop these positive qualities, people will have trust in you and trust is the major key to success in life and in successful relationships with others.

Real integrity stays in place whether the test is adversity or prosperity.

INTEGRITY

It cannot be bought and it cannot be measured in money. It is a prerequisite in determining the fibre and character of an individual and an organization. Integrity demands that there be no twilight zone—something is either right or it is wrong; black or it is white. Principles may be inborn ethics or, sometimes, mandated. But integrity requires scourging moral courage, magnetized by a fervor for an ideal. The complete person is a union of unswerving integrity, pulsating energy, and rugged determination—and the greatest of these is integrity. One individual with integrity is a majority.

To reflect integrity is to invite trust. To possess integrity is to command respect. Integrity is found in simple issues and those complex. Its presence is critical. It demands total loyalty, a commitment to cause, a dedication to mission, an unflagging determination. Morals, Ethics, Standards, and Integrity— from these flow a torrent of values. Deeds, not words. It is clear that what you do and what you are speak with deafening impact, not what you say you are. Honesty isn't the best policy. It is the only policy: for an individual and an organization, integrity isn't a sometimes thing. It is everything.

R. ARMSTRONG

IMAGINATION

Broken Illusion

One cold winter night two travelers searched down a lonely road for a resting place. There were no motels and the only thing they found was an abandoned farmhouse. They were very tired so they decided to pull in and sleep there for the night. Inside it was very dark but they were able to find an old rusting bed covered with a lumpy mattress in an upstairs bedroom. As they lay down and closed their eyes the first man said, "I can't sleep without fresh air. Open the window." The second man tried to open a window in the room, but it was stuck. "I can't sleep without fresh air," the first man explained, "so break the window." The second man took off his shoe and broke the glass. This satisfied the first man who could now feel the fresh air. So the two men lay down and slept through the night without interruption.

The next morning when the two awoke, they discovered that the glass from the window had not been broken at all. Instead, the glass in the door of an old broken-down bookcase next to the window lay shattered all over the floor. No fresh air had come in at all, but because the first man believed there was fresh air, he was able to sleep comfortably. Nothing had changed in his situation except what he had perceived in his mind. His fears were only creations of his own imagination.

Some of the greatest minds of the past and present have achieved the extraordinary and turned their dreams into reality by harnessing the creative power of imagination. George Bernard Shaw wrote, "Imagination is the beginning of creation. You imagine what you desire; you will what you imagine; and at last, you create what you will." Imagination involves seeing things not simply as they are now, but as they can be. Several years ago an experiment was conducted with a high school basketball team demonstrating how creative imagination can improve performance at anything you do. Students of roughly equal ability were divided into three groups to test their skills at free-throw shots.

The first group practiced throwing free-throws for twenty minutes, every day for a month. The second group, the control group of the experiment, did not practice at all. The third group practiced their free-throws in their imagination for twenty minutes a day for a month. At the end of the experiment the results showed that the first group improved their average by twenty-four percent. The second group showed no improvement at all. The third group through their use of mental rehearsal, improved by twenty-three percent! By practicing in their imagination they improved their results.

Your imagination is a powerhouse. It can be used to work for you or against you. If you fill your mind with thoughts of fear, doubt, defeat, and uncertainty then the results you produce will be undesirable. On the other hand, your creative imagination can help you visualize solutions to difficult problems, create new ideas, and project a mental image of you succeeding at achieving your goals. By creating a desire first in your mental world it then becomes possible to create it in your physical world. Picture yourself vividly as accomplishing your desires and that alone will contribute immeasurably to your success.

THOUGHTS ARE THINGS

I hold it true that thoughts are things;
They're endowed with bodies and breath and wings:
And that we send them forth to fill
The world with good results, or ill.
That which we call our secret thought
Speeds forth to earth's remotest spot,
Leaving its blessings or its woes
Like tracks behind it as it goes.

We build our future, thought by thought,
For good or ill, yet know it not.
Yet so the universe was wrought.
Thought is another name for fate;
Choose then thy destiny and wait,
For love brings love and hate brings hate.

HENRY VAN DYKE

INFLUENCE

For Sale by Owner

Many times when you set out to accomplish your goals and dreams, people, including your friends and family, will have a strong influence on your decision to move forward. The next time you have an original idea, share it with people you know. Often, they will begin listing several reasons why it won't work. Many of them, by nature, are just trying to protect you. They want you to be aware of all the pitfalls. And they truly are, in their own way, trying to be helpful. But, sometimes this makes you question yourself and your abilities and soon your idea or goal has lost its appeal.

Once there was a man who lived by the side of the road and sold hot dogs. He was hard of hearing so he had no radio. He had trouble with his eyes so he read no newspapers. But he sold good hot dogs. He put up a sign on the highway telling how good they were. Each day, he would stand by the side of the road and shout, "Buy the best hot dog you've ever had." And people bought. They bought a lot. So he increased his meat and roll orders. He also bought a bigger stove to take care of his trade. He got his son home from college to help him. But then something happened. His son said, "Dad, haven't you been listening to the radio? If money stays tight we are bound to have bad business. Haven't you been reading the paper? Times are tough, there may be a recession. You had better prepare for poor business." Whereupon the father thought, "Well, my son has gone to college. He reads the papers and he listens to the radio, and he ought to know."

So the father cut down on his meat and roll orders. He took down the advertising signs. And he no longer bothered to stand by the road selling hot dogs. And his hot dog sales fell almost overnight. "You're right son," the father said to the boy. "We certainly are headed for tough times."

When you are working toward your goals, or considering trying something you have never done before, you must first believe in yourself. Because we are so strongly influenced by those we care about, it is important to get them to work for you instead of against you. Allow them to help you evaluate both sides of the picture instead of looking only at the dark side. Above all, do what you feel is the right thing to do. Some people may say that it is unrealistic to avoid thinking of certain negative aspects of any undertaking. The best way to evaluate your objective is list the positive and negative considerations of any proposed goal. Then, by eliminating the negative points, one by one, only the positive points remain. If you listen to people who think in negative terms, it can sabotage your objective and cause your thinking to become negative.

There is an old Latin proverb that states, "If you always live with those that limp, you will yourself learn to limp." Once you realize just how much effect your current circle of friends and those you associate with have on your way of thinking you can understand the truth in that statement. Be careful not to allow the negativism of others to inhibit your personal growth and your potential for success.

LIKE OUR ASSOCIATES

The water placed in a goblet, bowl or cup
Changes its form to its receptacle;
And so our plastic souls take various shapes
And characters of good or ill, to fit
The good or evil in the friends we choose.
Therefore, be ever careful in your choice of friends,
And let your special love be given to those
Whose strength of character may prove the whip
That drives you ever to fair wisdom's goal.

MUSHITO

IT'S UP TO ME

I get discouraged now and then when there are clouds of gray,
Until I think about the things that happened yesterday.
I do not mean the day before, or those months ago.
But all the yesterdays in which I had a chance to grow.
I think of opportunities that I allowed to fall aside
And those I took advantage of before they passed me by.
And I remember that the past presented quite a plight.
But somehow I endured it and the future seemed all right.
And I remind myself that I am capable and free,
And my success and happiness are really up to me.

JAMES J. METCALFE

POTENTIAL

Cash In on Your Potential

M ost of us live too near the surface of our abilities, dreading to call upon our deeper resources. Each one of us possesses unlimited talents, skills and abilities that are invaluable. If you don't know how to unlock them, you will never discover your true greatness.

A story is told of the Apaches in the time of the Old West. One day, the Apaches attacked a cavalry unit and captured the army paymaster's safe. They had never seen a safe before, but they knew it held a large amount of gold. But, there was one problem. They had no idea how to open the safe. They pounded on its knob with stones, whacked at it with their tomahawks, roasted it in a hot fire, soaked it in the river, and even tried blasting it open with gunpowder, but nothing seemed to work. Finally, the Apache chief had an idea. "Throw it off the cliff," he shouted to his men. This would surely break open the safe when it hit the rocks hundreds of feet below. Much to their disappointment, however, it did not work. All that happened was that one of the wheels broke off the safe.

Totally frustrated, they gave up and left the treasured safe in the ravine. Later, members of the army found the safe, and within a few minutes with the correct combination, opened the safe and found the gold still inside.

Many of us are like that safe. To find the treasures that lie deep inside of you, the right combination must first be found. Once unlocked, you will find the great untapped reserves of potential. To release your vast fortune of talent and abilities you must first make a commitment to cast from your mind all self-limiting thoughts forever. This can be achieved by the use of positive affirmation.

Each day you should affirm to yourself the wonderful powers and possibilities within you waiting to be utilized. You can never open the great resources that lie within you by allowing thoughts of worry, fear and despair to occupy your mind. With the right combination of ambition, confidence, determination, and enthusiasm you will unlock many doors that would otherwise stay closed. Professor William James, the eminent American psychologist, observed that, "Compared to what we ought to be, we are only half awake. We are making use of only a small part of our physical and mental resources."

Your potential is limited only by your belief in yourself. Your self-concept and belief about what you are and what you can be precisely determine *what you will be*. Begin digging deep within yourself to discover and then draw upon your tremendous wealth of untapped ability and potential. You will find that what you have to offer the world is every bit worth its weight in gold!

ME

Today I had a battle, the fight was hard and long;
My opponent was so stubborn, and I knew him to be wrong.
We didn't need a referee, because, when we were through,
The decision was unquestioned, nor did we start anew.
I never did like fighting, and yet I fail to see,
How I could help but cheer a bit, when I had conquered ME.

HAZEL V. WOLFE

BELIEVE IN YOURSELF

Believe in yourself! Believe you were made
To do any task without calling for aid.
Believe, without growing too scornfully proud,
That you, as the greatest and least are endowed.
A mind to do thinking and potential to be wise,
To overcome obstacles no matter their size.
Believe in yourself! You're divinely designed
And perfectly made for the work of mankind.
This truth you must cling to through danger and pain;
The heights man has reached you can also attain.
Believe to the very last hour, for it's true,
That whatever you will you've been gifted to do.
The wisdom of ages is yours if you'll read
But you've got to believe in yourself to succeed.

EDGAR A. GUEST

SELF-ESTEEM

Convinced of Greatness

A story is told of a young man named Bunker Bean who was tricked into believing in himself. Bunker was a man who was penniless, orphaned as a child, and had an enormous inferiority complex. As an adult, he lived in a cheap boarding house suffering a life of frustration, fear, low self-esteem, and poverty. There he meet a spiritualistic medium who preached reincarnation, and had convinced him to give up part of his wages in exchange for psychic readings. After much fanfare and theatrics, the psychic revealed to Bunker that he had once been the great Napoleon Bonaparte, Emperor of France. The psychic told Bunker that life progressed in vast karmic cycles and although Bunker's life was very negative, he was completing the lower half of the cycle.

The upcoming portion of his life was to be the exact opposite and he was to take on the successful qualities of Napoleon. Bunker believed the psychic and began assuming the virtues of his new role model. Just thinking of himself as Napoleon made Bunker feel like a million dollars. He stood upright and studied himself in the mirror. He felt a great wave of confidence surge within him. And he became such a success that his friends and employer could hardly believe the changes.

But one day something happened. He found out that the psychic was a total fake and everything he had told Bunker was untrue. The shock was at first devastating, but because he had acquired winning habits which had become such a part of him, it didn't matter. He had learned the meaning of a great truth: "We become what we think about." Or as Benjamin Franklin stated, "We should practice what we wish to become, not what we are."

Unfortunately, many people pass through life selling themselves short. Bunker realized that when he *did not* believe that he was somebody, he was not; but when *he did* believe that he was somebody, *he was*. By changing his attitude about himself, he became wealthy and successful along with gaining prestige and respect from others. When you feel good about yourself, and believe in your talents and skills, nothing can stop you. You will discover your true greatness as soon as you begin to *feel* and see yourself as a *great person*.

Your achievements, effectiveness and creativity are governed to a large extent by how you feel about yourself and how you see yourself as being. To build high self-esteem you must recognize the mental picture you hold of yourself and of your abilities. If you have feelings of inferiority, visualize in your mind a mental picture of the type of person you would like to become with the attributes you wish to acquire. Remember, *we are not what we think we are, rather, <u>what we think—we are</u>*.

SPRING CLEAN YOUR SELF-ESTEEM

Keep Learning: Learn something new every day, even if it's only a new word, a little known fact, or the name of a new co-worker.

Choose Your Friends Carefully: Cultivate relationships with people who make you feel important and whose accomplishments you admire. Avoid anybody who puts you down. Do not spend time with people who are bad for your mental health.

Build Skills: Do something every day that you do well. No matter how insignificant it may seem, any accomplishment bolsters self-esteem.

Change Yourself: Change those things about yourself that bother you. If you can't do anything about them, stop brooding. Never Give Up: Never, never, never give up. The only thing that stands between mediocrity and excellence, between failure and success, is the little voice within you that says, "I can do it."

Positive Self Talk: Speak to yourself kindly. Do not focus on your mistakes, just understand that there was a better way to do it, and promise yourself that next time you will do it differently.

Go For It: Take risks. A single courageous act is the first step on the road to enduring self-confidence.

Keep Your Perspective: Mistakes are not catastrophes. Acknowledge your shortcomings and remember that you can never be a failure as long as you have given your best effort.

Be Realistic: Set goals realistic enough to be attained, yet difficult enough to be a challenge. Reaching your goals, no matter how small, will give you a tremendous amount of self-esteem.

Physical Fitness: Aerobic exercise enhances feelings of positive well-being and zest for life—major components of self-esteem. The discipline involved in exercising will translate into other areas of your life, helping you shape up your work, personal relationships as well as your body.

Look Good, Feel Good: Take care of yourself. Low self-esteem sometimes begins with a dissatisfaction about appearance, so take time to look your best as often as you can. It will help make you feel good about yourself.

SELF-IMPROVEMENT

Keep Sharpening Your Axe

It has been said that the biggest room in the world is the room of self-improvement. Abraham Lincoln stated, "I will study and prepare myself and someday my chance will come."

An old story tells of two woodsmen cutting trees in the forest. The first woodsman attacked the trees relentlessly. As soon as one tree started to fall, he would rush over to the next one and start chopping furiously. Eager to cut down as many trees as possible, he worked all day without taking any breaks or even stopping for lunch. He started earlier in the morning than the other woodsmen, and stayed later in the evening.

His fellow woodsmen marvelled at his fast pace throughout the day. At the end of the day, though, they were surprised to see that another woodsman had actually cut down more trees. He hadn't chopped quite as hard as the first woodsman, and he took regular breaks throughout the day. This puzzled them.

The eager woodsman walked over to the second woodsman and asked, "How could you have cut down more trees than me? I work harder, faster, and I started earlier and worked later. What is the secret to your success?" The second woodsman paused for a moment and said, "Well, there is no secret to my success, but I can tell you this. No matter how busy I am or how hard I may be working, I always stop and take time to sharpen my axe. Because when your axe is sharp, you can chop more wood with less effort." Self-improvement means sharpening your axe. It means taking the time to subject yourself to a rigid self-examination in all areas of your life. Once you have determined those areas in which you feel a need for improvement and development, you can then proceed to substitute the weak qualities you've found with the qualities that will distinguish greatness of mind, spirit, and character. Knowing precisely what you are now and what you intend to be is the first step in self-improvement. As Socrates advised us, "Know thyself."

There are several ways you can achieve continual growth and personal improvement. One way is to start building a success library. Some of the world's greatest thinkers and leaders have written about the psychology of success and personal achievement. Reading books that motivate and inspire you will act as stimuli toward continued growth which in turn will empower you to greatness. Listening to personal growth tapes is another way to be uplifted and empowered to excel to be your best. You can turn a ten-thousand dollar automobile into a hundred-thousand dollar rolling university by listening to educational and motivational tapes while driving to and from work each day.

Attending seminars and workshops on personal development is yet another powerful way to learn the fundamentals of success and winning. Nourishing your mind is the best investment you can ever make; no one can take it away from you. It will be worth all the time, money, and energy you may spend. It is important that you do something every day that will improve your mind and the quality of your life. If you want to have the edge in your personal and professional life, you must always take time out each day to *sharpen your axe.*

THEY WAIT TOO LONG

Some people wait too long in life
To use their clever brains.
And then they find it is too late
To make impressive gains.
They will not take the time to get
The knowledge they require
To reach the glorious success
To which their hearts aspire.

For they would rather have their fun
And play around today,
Than try to reach a certain goal
That seems so far away.
The value of their dream in life
Is something that they measure
In terms of idle wanderings
And moments made for pleasure.

And strange as it may seem,
they have The nerve to weep and wail
And wonder why with all their brains
Their feeble efforts fail.

JAMES J. METCALFE

T E A M W O R K

The Tie That Binds

A manager of a small manufacturing plant was having problems with one of his employees. The employee always seemed to keep to himself and was often aloof around his co-workers. During the company's weekly meetings, the employee never participated in sharing his opinion on how things around the plant could be improved. When given a project to work on, the employee never asked his fellow employees for their help or advice. During group projects, the employee preferred to work alone at his work station.

One day the manager called the employee into his office. "I have called you into my office today to impress upon you the importance of teamwork here at the plant," the manager explained. "The quality and effectiveness of our work here depends on all of us working together as a team to produce the best quality products that we can manufacture. It's not the work of one, but the cooperative effort of many that allows us to accomplish this goal." The manager then opened the drawer of his desk and pulled out a pencil, handed it to the employee, and said, "Take this pencil and break it for me." The employee took the pencil and snapped it in two with ease. "Now," asked the manager, "how many co-workers work in your department?" The employee responded, "Fifteen, sir." The manager again reached into his desk and this time pulled out fifteen pencils grouped together with a rubber band. The manager then said, "Take these pencils and try to break them in the same fashion that you broke the first." The employee tried as he might, but could not break the group of pencils. "Do you see my point?" the manager asked. "Teamwork, doing things together," the manager explained, "is what makes this company strong and unstoppable, but if we stand divided, we can fail at our objectives and our goals will be easily broken."

Every manager in the corporate world as well as every coach on the playing field has held pep talks to instilled the value of teamwork. Teamwork is the ability to work together toward a common vision. Through cooperation and harmony, teamwork is the binding force necessary for success in any organization. Through this cooperative effort the entire group generates an energy of creative effectiveness. It divides not the people, but the task at hand, and doubles the success toward the desired objective.

Group effort enables each of its team members to accomplish far more than one person could achieve alone. Teamwork means that Together Everyone Achieves More. And when the "team" gives their best and accomplishes the task, each individual on the team feels like a winner. Get involved in developing a motivating environment through team work. Working together means winning together. Pitch in, share your talents and enjoy the rewards of winning.

Build for your team a feeling of oneness, of dependence upon one another and of strength to be derived by unity.

VINCE LOMBARDI

TEAMWORK

It's all very well to have courage and skill and it's fine to be counted a star.
But the single deed with its touch of thrill does not tell the players you are:
For there is no lone hand in the game we play,
we must work to a bigger scheme.
And the thing that counts in the world is
"How do you pull with the team?"

They may sound your praise and call you great,
they may single you out for fame.
But you must work with your running mate or you'll never win the game.
Oh, never the work of life is done by the one with a selfish dream,
for the battle is lost or the battle is won by the spirit of the team.

You may think it fine to be praised for skill, but a greater thing to do is to
set your mind and set your will on the goal that's just in view.
It is helping your fellow players to score when their chances hopeless seem.
It is forgetting self 'til the game is over and fighting for the team.

EDGAR A. GUEST

A SHORT COURSE IN WORK RELATIONS

The six most important words:
I admit I was wrong.
The five most important words:
You did a great job.
The four most important words:
What do you think?
The three most important words:
Could you please...
The two most important words:
Thank you.
The most important word:
We.

ANONYMOUS

TIME MANAGEMENT

Worth Banking On

I f you had a bank that credited your account each morning with $86,400, that carried over no balance from day to day, allowed you to keep no cash in your account, and every evening withdrew whatever part of the amount you had failed to use during the day, what would you do? Draw out every cent of course!

Well, you have such a bank and its name is "Time." Every morning it credits you with 86,400 seconds. Each night it rules off, as lost, whatever of these you have failed to invest to good purpose. It carries over no balances. It allows no overdrafts. Each day it opens a new account with you. Each night it burns the records of the day. If you fail to use the day's deposits the loss is yours. There is no drawing against the "Tomorrow." You must live, in the present— on today's deposit. You must invest in your time wisely in order to receive the benefits of health, happiness and success.

One of the key components to success is the proper use of your time. The misuse of time is often the greatest cause of unhappiness and failure. Developing your time awareness means making the time to do the things most important to you. Usually the dividing line between success and failure can by expressed in five words: "*I did not have time.*" Taking charge of your life means that you assume total responsibility for managing your time. Many times we feel that there is just never enough time to do the things we want to do. Have you ever tried to dig a hole in dry beachsand? The faster you dig, the faster new sand falls in to replace what you had just dug out. Trying to catch up with all of the things that need to be done in our 'always on the go' lives is similar. New things will always appear that are added to your list along with the old things. When faced with this situation the best strategy is to become a time-management expert. Time management is life management.

Try keeping a to-do list for each day. Write one out the night before or first thing in the morning and prioritize your activities. Start with your number one priority and work on it until you finish. Then go to the next one. If you don't finish everything on your list, don't worry. You at least accomplished those things that were most important. This list will keep you focused on what needs to be done and keep you from wasting time on doing little things of unimportance.

Another way to manage your time is to be ruthless with time wasters. Avoid people who waste their time on activities that deviate from your goals and what you want to accomplish. Also, during the day stop and ask yourself these questions: "Is what I'm doing now the best use of my time?" "Am I doing something that is bringing me closer to my goals and where I want to be?"

Tomorrow's success is the result of today's planning. Failing to plan is planning to fail. You can't increase your time, but you can increase the value of your time. Master the success habit of managing your time more effectively. Also, learn to identify signs of procrastination or "Someday I'll" syndrome. Develop a mind-set that judges your every activity in terms of whether it brings you closer to your goals. Most people get ahead during the time others waste. Let the minutes of each day count in your favor.

GETTING THINGS DONE

The world has always cried out for men and women who get things done, for people who are self-starters and who see a task through to its finish.

It isn't how much you know, but what you get done that the world rewards and remembers.

More people are held back from success because they don't know how to get things done than for any other single reason.

The biggest handicap to success in not a lack of brains, nor a lack of character, nor a lack of willingness. It is weakness in getting things done.

This large group of people know what to do, and almost do it on time. They almost win promotions. They almost become leaders. They may miss by only a minute or an inch, but they do miss until they learn how to gain that minute or inch for themselves.

The almosts are not lazy. Often they are more busy than the very effective few. They putter around fuzzily all day long and half the night, though they fail to accomplish much.

They are held back by indecision, by a lack of organization in their work, and by overattention to minor details.

They are swirled around in circles and they get nowhere because they don't chart a straight course and then stick to it.

We don't need to work harder, we need to work more effectively. We must learn to make our work count.

It is the producers who raise the world's standard of living.

It is the producers who win the big share of the world's rewards. The producers have formed the habit of getting things done, and will not permit the "almosts" to get them off course.

WORK

No Bones About It

In just about every organization you will find four types of bones. First, there are the *wishbones*. These individuals spend a majority of their time wishing others would do the work. If they would just spend as much time working as they do wishing, more work would get done. Then, we have the *jawbones*. Needless to say, these are the ones who spend a lot of time talking about the work that needs to be done, but they never get anything done because they're always talking. The *knucklebones* love to knock what everyone else is doing. They usually don't put in much effort at work because their effort is poured into criticizing others. The most productive bones are the *backbones*. They get the work done and aren't concerned with who gets the credit. They like what they do, their work is exciting and challenging, and they never voice a distaste toward their employer or the people they work with. The backbone is a team player and there's *no bones about it*.

Consider the fact that we spend more than a third of our waking hours on the job. What environment would need to exist at your workplace for you to feel a sense of total job satisfaction? What can you contribute to your workplace that would allow you to be happy, content, and more productive? Peak performers are those people dedicated to their jobs. They enjoy what they do. Peak performers don't really consider what they do as "work" but as a labor of love with a total commitment to perform at their maximum best. As Will

Rogers observed, "What you're doing ain't work unless you would rather be doing something else." Your attitude and how you feel about your job is the underlining factor to your success as well as the success of your organization. Every workplace has its share of challenges, but the important thing to remember is that **you** are the backbone to your organization.

Consider the following memorandum. The (e) key was not functioning properly when it was typed. This will emphasize the importance of your contribution and commitment at work.

Xvxn though my typxwritxr is an old modxl, it works vxry wxll—xxcxpt for onx kxy. You would think that with all thx othxr kxys functioning propxrly, onx kxy not working would hardly bx noticxd; but just onx kxy out of whack sxxms to ruin thx wholx xffort. You may say to yoursxlf—Wxll, I'm only onx pxrson. No onx will noticx if I don't do my bxst. But it doxs makx a diffxrxncx bxcausx to bx xffxctive an organization nxxds activx participation by xvxry onx to thx bxst of his or hxr ability. So thx nxxt timx you think you arx not important, rxmxmbxr this old typxwritxr. You arx a kxy pxrson.

You can see that the quality of work is compromised when only one person (e) is not working at their best. Happiness at work comes from doing something you enjoy doing. Something you care about, something that totally absorbs you. If you are not happy at work then maybe it's time to make a change. If you are happy at your job then commit to giving the best of yourself. You are an important **key** to the success of your organization. As an employee you are the backbone of the company and there's *no bones about it*!

WANTED

A person for hard work and rapid promotion; someone who can find things to be done without the help of a manager and three assistants.

A person who gets to work on time in the morning and does not imperil the lives of others in an attempt to be the first out of the office at night.

A person who listens carefully when they are spoken to and asks only enough questions to ensure the accurate carrying out of instructions.

A person who moves quickly and makes as little noise as possible about it.

A person who looks you straight in the eye and tells the truth every time.

A person who enjoys their work and does not whine for having to work.

A person who is neat in appearance.

A person who does not sulk for an hour's overtime in emergencies.

A person who is cheerful, courteous to everyone, and determined to make good.

This person is wanted everywhere. Age or lack of experience does not count. There isn't any limit, except his or her own ambition, to the number or size of the jobs he or she can get. This person is wanted in every business. Are you that person?

How we think shows through in how we act.
Attitudes are mirrors of the mind. They reflect thinking.

DAVID J. SCHWARTZ

Whenever you possess conviction and belief about something,
you will experience it. Belief creates the actual fact.

WILLIAM JAMES

For good or bad, your conversation is your advertisement.
Every time you open your mouth you let someone look into your mind.
As is our confidence, so is our capacity.

WILLIAM HAZLITT

The quality of a persons life is in direct proportion to their commitment to excellence.

VINCE LOMBARDI

What you get by reaching your goals is not nearly as important
as what you become along the way.

What is now proved was once only imagined.
Only those who can see the invisible can do the impossible!

Our past is not our potential.

Form a good opinion of yourself and then deserve the good opinion of others.

Self-improvement is the night school and the day school that requires no tuition.
It's the greatest university, the best college in this country.
You can do more for yourself than anyone else can, or,
to put it perfectly plainly, more than anyone else will.

Those who make the worst use of their time are the same ones
who complain that there is never enough time.

Some of us will do our jobs well and some will not,
but we will all be judged by only one thing—the result.

VINCE LOMBARDI

CHAPTER 4

THE LIGHT *of* WISDOM

THE ROAD IS ALWAYS BETTER

"*The road is always better than the inn.*" These words by the great Spanish writer, Cervantes, mean a way of living. In my younger days I often aimed too hard to reach some goal, finish some job. "When this is done," I'd say, "I shall find real satisfaction and reward." But later I came to realize that each achievement, like each inn, is only a point along the road. The real goodness of living comes with the journey itself, with the striving and desire to keep moving. Now I find that I can look back on my eighty-four years with pleasure and, what is even more important to me, that I can still look to the future with hope and desire. I have learned to take each inn along the way with a traveler's stride—not as a stopping point, but a starting point for some new and better endeavor.

MAURICE MAETERLINCK

AWARENESS

Lost and Found

Many years ago, before electric refrigerators replaced iceboxes, the manager of a local ice house lost his watch of great sentimental value. All employees searched for the watch, but no one could find it. Finally the manager posted signs all over town offering a substantial reward to anyone who found his watch.

The next day a young boy rode up to the icehouse on his bicycle and asked if he could look for the watch. The manager said, "Don't bother me, boy!" But the boy was insistent. Finally the manager told him, "Look boy, we can't have you underfoot while we're moving these big blocks of ice. You can come back on Thursday afternoon when everyone is gone." Meanwhile, the search continued, but the watch failed to materialize.

On Thursday afternoon the young boy came back to look for the watch. The manager lead him into the dark, cold room, and ten minutes later the boy returned with the watch to claim his reward. The manager was amazed. He asked, "How did you find the watch? Nobody else could find it and we've gone over every inch of this place. How did you do it?" The boy replied, "It was easy. All I did was listen for the tick."

Often we are so preoccupied with normal activities of daily life that we fail to look for the many opportunities that surround us. Also we fail to stop and listen to our inner feelings of self-worth. Awareness is keeping alert to all that goes on around you.

Becoming aware of the people, your surroundings, and of the activities you are doing enables you to enjoy and appreciate your total life experience. This means striving to stretch the range of eye and ear and taking time to look and listen and comprehend. Your awareness is the degree of clarity with which you perceive, understand, and evaluate, both consciously and unconsciously, everything that affects your life. You then act in accordance with your present level of awareness. Developing your awareness enables you to make the most of each moment as it occurs through keen consciousness, attentiveness, vigilance, and responsiveness.

Self-awareness is knowing the truth about yourself. It is understanding your own creative abilities and unrestricted potential. Self-awareness is being consciously aware of everything you think, say, do and feel. It is an inner knowing of all your values, concepts, beliefs, and assumptions.

As a total person you become aware and take full responsibility for your behavior and actions. Your increased understanding of yourself makes it possible to fulfill your potentials for growth. Before you can improve upon your self-awareness, you have to take the advice of Marcus Aurelius who advised us to, "Look within."

Ask yourself such questions as: What do I like best about myself? What do I like least about myself? What price am I willing to pay for excellence and success, and to become the most I can become as a human being? What are my talents? What are my interests? What do I believe in? What things are most important to me? What kind of person am I?

Take the time to develop your awareness. Stop and listen to the ticking of your inner self and have a clear understanding of what you stand for and who you are.

THE ART OF AWARENESS

Thoreau wrote: "Only that day dawns to which we are awake."

The art of awareness is the art of learning how to wake up to the eternal miracle of life with its limitless possibilities.

It is developing the deep sensitivity through which you may suffer and know tragedy, but through which you also experience the grandeur of human life.

It is developing a sense of oneness with all life.

It is identifying yourself with the hopes, dreams, fears, and longings of others, that you may understand them and help them.

It is learning to interpret the thoughts, feelings, and moods of others through their words, tones, inflections, facial expressions, and movements.

It is keeping mentally alert to all that goes on around you; it is being curious, observant, imaginative that you may build an ever increasing fund of knowledge of the universe.

It is searching for beauty everywhere, in a flower, a mountain, a machine, a sonnet, and symphony.

It is knowing wonder, awe, and humility in the face of life's unexplained mysteries.

It is discovering the mystic powers of the silence and coming to know the secret inner voice of intuition.

It is avoiding blind spots in considering problems and situations; it is striving "to see life steadily and see it whole."

It is enlarging the scope of your life through the expansion of your personality.

Through a growing awareness you see all that life has to offer.

W. A. PETERSON

CHANGE

Time to Move On

There once was a man who lived at the same farmhouse all his life. It was a good home, but with the passing years, the man began to tire of it. He longed for a change, for something better. As the days passed, he found a new reason to criticize the old place. Finally, he decided to sell, and listed the farm house with a real estate broker who promptly prepared a sales advertisement. The ad emphasized, as one might expect, all the home's advantages: ideal location out in the country, modern equipment, acres of fertile ground, healthy live stock, etc. Before placing the ad in the newspaper, the realtor called the man on the phone and read the ad copy to him for his approval. When he had finished, the man cried out, "Hold everything! I've changed my mind. I am not going to sell. I've been looking for a place like that all my life."

Many of us may agree with the statement, "If it ain't broke, don't fix it." But even when we feel that things are just fine we have to look beyond where we are today and believe that a positive change in our life will expose us to better opportunities in the future. The key to making life meaningful lies in one's ability to adapt to change. Most change is met with some form of resistance. We are creatures of certainty. Many times we feel uncomfortable about change because it involves dealing with the unknown, going from the familiar to the unfamiliar. Change causes us to look back on what we had, fearing to lose it, rather than looking forward to the opportunities of the future.

As the saying goes, "Can't live with it, can't live without it." Often times change involves risk. It means stepping outside your comfort zone and into the unfamiliar zone. Change is a fact of life. Accepting change enables an individual to grow and discover new experiences. Change provokes a feeling of fear which can affect your attitude and ability to be flexible and adaptable. Until you reach the point that you perceive the pain of changing something in your life to be less painful than the pain of leaving things the way they are, you will be reluctant to do things differently. It is when you get sick and tired of being sick and tired, you'll then look at change from a different perspective.

To effectively manage change in your life you must first be willing to accept change as a challenge and step outside your comfort zone. The comfort zone is our personal area of activities and relationships in life with which we feel most comfortable or familiar. As you move beyond this imaginary zone experiencing something new and different, you feel resistance, fear, and apprehension. Once you can overcome these feelings and step outside of this self-limiting boundary you can then be exposed to new opportunities and personal growth. When you take this important step outside your comfort zone, you will then be exposed to all of the exciting experiences life has to offer. You may find that it's a place you've been looking for all your life.

There is one person to whom you can continually compare yourself, and profit greatly from the comparison: Compare yourself today to the person you were yesterday.

CONTROLS

You cannot control the length of your life, but you can control its width and depth.

You cannot control the contour of your countenance, but **you can** control its expression.

You cannot control the other person's opportunities, but **you can** grasp your own.

You cannot control the weather, but **you can** control the moral atmosphere which surrounds you.

You cannot control the distance that your head shall be above the ground, but **you can** control the height of the contents of your mind.

You cannot control the other persons faults, but **you can** see to it that you yourself do not develop or harbor provoking propensities.

Why worry about things you cannot control? Get busy controlling the things that depend on you.

DECISIONS

A Quenching Decision

E very day you are faced with many important decisions to make. The outcome of these decisions will ultimately shape your destiny. They determine who you become and where you go in life. Can you think of a decision you made or failed to make that has strongly influenced your life today? It is the decisions you make today, not the current conditions in your life, that will lay the foundation for your future. You create the world you dream of with every choice you make. Realize the power behind your choice of a single decision and make a decision today, followed by an immediate action, to improve the quality of your life in a positive way.

One day a thirsty traveler was wandering through the desert and discovered a pump sticking out from the ground. As he approached what he thought was an illusion, he noticed a tin can attached to the handle. Inside was a note that explained that buried nearby was a jar of water to be used for priming the old pump. The note explained that, "You've got to give a little to get a lot. There's enough water in the jar to prime the pump but not if you drink some first. After you're done, fill the jar and put it back like you found it for the next person." Quickly, the traveler located the buried jar, and stood before the pump. He was now faced with a very important decision. Whether to drink the water that he was holding in his hand and satisfy his immediate thirst, or to take a chance that the small amount of water invested would prime the pump and offer him an unlimited supply of fresh, cool water.

As you can see, this thirsty traveler had a very important decision to make. Indecision would not allow him to go any further than where he was. His choice, at that moment, would make a major impact on his life. It was important for him to understand not only the immediate effect of his decision, but also how it would affect him in the future.

Some people think that making no decision at all is a decision in its own way. These people fall short of their goals because they are afraid to make a decision and stick by it. You, on the other hand, understand what a powerful thing choice is—the power to select. It is one of the main things that can change your life almost in an instant. You are making choices every minute of the day, and upon every choice something important depends. Your world revolves around each choice and decision you make.

At every point in your life there are alternatives, and you have to choose between them, whether you want to or not. You choose your attitude toward life, either positive or negative; You choose whether you will grasp opportunity when it is presented to you; you choose whether you will work at developing your greatness; you choose to commit yourself to continual self-improvement; and you decide what kind of life you will live.

Life is shaped by minor decisions. Today, begin priming the pump of your career, relationships, health, and future. Make a bold decision right now about how you can change these areas of your life to quench your thirst for a more fulfilling life.

Does the course of action you plan to follow seem logical and reasonable? Never mind what anyone else has to say, does it make sense to you? If it does, it is probably right.

Does it pass the test of sportsmanship? In other words, if everyone followed this same course of action would the results be beneficial for all?

Where will your plan of action lead? How will it affect others? What will it do to you?

Will you think well of yourself when you look back at what you have done?

Try to separate yourself from the problem at hand. Imagine, for a moment, it is the problem of the person you most admire. Ask yourself how that person would handle it.

Hold up the final decision to the glaring light of publicity. Would you want your family and friends to know what you have done? The decisions we make in the hope that no one will find out are usually wrong.

HARRY E. FOSDICK

WHEN YOU CHANGE YOUR THINKING

you change your beliefs;
When you change your beliefs,
you change your expectations;
When you change your expectations,
you change your attitude;
When you change your attitude,
you change your behavior;
When you change your behavior,
you change your performance;
When you change your performance,
YOU CHANGE YOUR LIFE!

EXPECTATION

Soaking in Uncertainty

A man, driving down a lonely country road one dark and rainy night, had a flat tire. He stepped out of his car and opened the trunk to get the spare and began changing the tire. He quickly learned that their was no lug wrench. A feeling of despair began to fill his mind. He looked up and noticed a light dimly up the road coming from a farmhouse. So he set out on foot through the driving rain.

"Surely someone at the house would have a lug wrench I could borrow, but then again they may not," he thought to himself. "It is late at night and everyone is probably asleep in their warm, dry beds. Maybe they won't answer the door. And even if they do, they will surely be angry at being awakened in the middle of the night."

The man continued picking his way blindly in the dark. By now his shoes and clothing were soaked. His mind continued to be filled with low expectation. "Even if someone does answer the door," he thought to himself, "they will probably shout something like, what's the big idea waking everyone up at this hour!" This thought made him very angry. "What right does someone have to refuse me the loan of a lug wrench? After all, here I am stranded in the middle of nowhere, soaked to the skin. These people are no doubt unfriendly and selfish, there's no doubt about that!"

The man finally reached the house, and banged loudly on the door. The lights went on inside, and a window opened above. "Who is it?" a voice called out. "You know darn well who it is," yelled the soaking visitor, his face white with anger. "It's me! You can keep your blasted lug wrench. I wouldn't borrow it now if you had the last one on earth!" He turned around and walked away.

Whatever you expect, backed with a strong belief and conviction, often becomes your own self-fulfilling prophecy. You predict a certain outcome and then behave in such a way as to fulfill and bring it into reality. You become your own fortune teller. It's not necessarily what you want in life, but what you <u>expect</u> from it. Put another way, life is like Christmas—you are more likely to get what you expect than what you want. When you have low expectations about people, situations, and your abilities to succeed you soon discover that you will seldom be disappointed.

Have you ever noticed that when someone shares bad news with you, it is often accompanied by the statement, "That's just what I was afraid of!" Or someone says, "I get sick this time every year" and guess what happens? They get sick the same time every year. When we fear that bad things might happen, they usually do! When we predict failure in something we try to do, we usually fail. Conversely, when we expect success from our lives, we usually succeed.

Many of us never rise above our negative expectations and become the high achievers that we are capable of becoming. High-achieving men and women continually draw on their confidence in themselves and believe in successful outcomes.

Begin today developing the attitude of positive expectation, an attitude of anticipating success in all areas of your life. It is a prophecy of what <u>can</u> and <u>will</u> happen.

YES I CAN!

If you think you are beaten, you are;
If you think you dare not, you don't!
If you want to win, but think you can't
   It is almost certain you won't.
If you think you'll lose, you've lost;
   For out in the world we find
Success begins with a person's will;
   It's all in the state of mind.
If you think you are outclassed you are,
   You've got to think high to rise.
You've got to be sure of yourself before
   You can ever win the prize.
Life's battles don't always go
   To the stronger woman or man,
But sooner or later the one who wins
Is the one who believes that they can.

WALTER D. WINTLE

GROWTH

Rising Above Yesterday

Your achievements today are the sum total of all your thoughts and actions of yesterday. You are today where these thoughts and actions have brought you and you will be tomorrow where the thoughts and actions of today take you. This is called the law of accumulation which states that everything that you think, do, and that which happens to you in life, counts. Vincent van Gogh stated, "Great things are not done by impulse but by a series of small things brought together." Day by day, every event and experience in your life is added to the sum total toward your personal growth. The story of the Chinese bamboo tree helps illustrate this point.

When the seed of the Chinese bamboo tree is planted, it is watered and fertilized regularly. During the first four years, there is no visible growth. However, during the fifth year when it finally emerges from the ground, it grows to a height of ninety feet in just six weeks. Plant experts say that during it's first four years in the soil, the bamboo seed is building an elaborate root system. It is this root system that enables it to grow ninety feet and allows the Chinese bamboo to stand sturdy and strong, all in just six weeks. Now, did the tree take five years to grow or was it only one year?

Personal growth, like the bamboo, is not a sudden change. You are not exactly the same person you were last month or last year. Every minute of each hour your natural function is growth; to expand mentally, spiritually and physically. Growth often necessitates giving up what we are familiar with for something yet unknown to us. You cannot develop your true potential by sticking to old habits and beliefs. Unless you try to do something beyond what you have already mastered, you will never grow.

When you are faced with daily life situations and experiences, they should be looked upon as a source of growth and positive change. The next time you are faced with a difficult situation affirm to yourself, "Good, now I can grow some more!" There is always a lesson you can take from these experiences and then use for your advancement.

POSITIVE GROWTH

If you find me stumbling and falling, I may just be trying something new—
I am learning.
If you find me sad it may be that I've just realized that I have been fooling myself and making the same stupid mistakes over and over again—
I am exploring.
If you find me terribly frightened, I may just be in a new situation—
I am reaching out.
If you find me crying, it may be because I failed—
I am trying.
If you find me very quiet, it may be that I am planning—
I will try again.
If you find me angry, I may have just discovered that I was not really trying—
I am erring.
If you find me with a strange self-satisfied smile,
I may have just discovered that I have everything I need for growing—
I am knowing.
If you find me ecstatically happy, I may have finally succeeded—
I am growing.

SOURCE: ARKANSAS REHABILITATION RESEARCH AND TRAINING CENTER

GROWING STRONGER

For every hill I've had to climb,
For every stone that bruised my feet,
For all the blood and sweet and grime,
For blinding storms and burning heat,
My heart sings but a grateful song—
These were the things that made me strong!

For all the heartaches and the tears,
For all the anguish and the pain,
For gloomy days and fruitless years,
And for the hopes that lived in vain,
I do give thanks, for now I know
These were the things that helped me grow!

It's not the softer things of life
Which stimulate one's will to strive;
But bleak adversity and strife,
Do most to keep one's will alive.
Over rose-strewn paths many creep,
But brave hearts dare to climb the steep.

AUTHOR UNKNOWN

KNOWLEDGE

Treading on Wisdom

D o you really have the burning desire to discover your true greatness and acquire the knowledge that will enable you to grow into the successful person that you are capable of becoming? You should always take the opportunity to upgrade your knowledge and learn more about those things that can help you move toward your dreams. One way to gain the knowledge of success is to read the countless books that have been written to assist us in unlocking our unlimited potential. Another way to gain the knowledge of success is to study successful men and women and then model their successful actions and behavior. You must cultivate an intense desire to learn and discover everything you can, from all sources, the knowledge that will enable you to effectively achieve your dreams.

The story is told of a young man who one day went to visit a wise old sage to ask him how he could gain knowledge of the secrets to success and happiness. The sage replied by asking the young man to walk with him to a nearby lake. As they approached the lake, the sage continued to walk out into the water. Not knowing what the old sage was doing, the young man followed. When the water got to be about four feet deep, the sage suddenly grabbed the young man and pushed his head under the water and continued to hold it there. After a very short time, the young man began to panic. He desperately struggled to get free. Finally, the old sage let him up. The young man was coughing and spluttering and grasping for air.

The old sage asked, "When you were under the water, what one thing did you want most of all?" Still trying to catch his breath, the young man explained, "I wanted air, you old fool!" The old sage said, "When you desire the knowledge you seek with the same intensity that you desired to breathe, then nothing will stop you from attaining it."

It has been said that knowledge is power. The truth is that applied knowledge is power. It's not how much knowledge you acquire that counts, but how you use it. It's not what you know but what you do with what you know that produces results. Your knowledge should be put to use in a way that will enrich your life and the lives of others. You have the ability to perform at exceptional levels in at least one area of your life, given that you activate your thought processes (mental muscles) through acquired knowledge. To move ahead of your current conditions, you must expand your current level of knowledge. Although we have the unlimited potential to learn, many of us use only a fraction of our minds. Studies show that the average person uses less than five percent of his or her mental abilities.

With all of the vast knowledge available to help us grow and become more successful in our lives, why is it that few of us take advantage of these resources? There is more information available on how to be successful in every area of life today than ever in history. Sadly only three percent of the population owns a library card! Statistics show that the average American reads fewer than one book per year and fifty-eight percent never finish a nonfiction book after high school. Think smarter, think bigger, and commit yourself to lifelong learning.

THE KNOWLEDGE OF LIFE

Life is a Gift...*accept it*;
Life is an Adventure...*dare it*;
Life is a Mystery...*unfold it*;
Life is a Game...*play it*;
Life is a Struggle...*face it*;
Life is Beauty...*praise it*;
Life is a Puzzle...*solve it*;
Life is an Opportunity...*take it*;
Life is a Challenge...*meet it*;
Life is Sorrowful...*overcome it*;
Life is a Song...*sing it*;
Life is a Goal...*achieve it*;
Life is a Duty...*perform it*;
Life is a Mission...*fulfill it*;
Life is Knowledge...*learn from it.*

AUTHOR UNKNOWN

You *create opportunity.* **You** develop the capacities for moving toward opportunity. **You** turn crises into creative opportunities and defeats into successes and frustration into fulfillment. With what? With your great invisible weapons: your good feelings about yourself, your determination to live the best life you can, and your feeling—that only you can give yourself—that you are a worth-while, deserving, person. You must fight for your right to fulfill the opportunity that God gave you to use your life well.

DR. MAXWELL MALTZ

THE SEARCH FOR SELF-RESPECT

OPPORTUNITY

Back Yard Opportunity

In a lecture given by Russell Conwell, founder of Temple University, he stated that, "If you wish to be great at all, you must begin where you are and with what you are now." He tells this story:

One day a traveler came along and told an old African farmer about people who had discovered diamond mines in Africa and had become very wealthy. Upon hearing this, the farmer became very excited and decided to sell off his farm and journey into Africa to find his own diamond mine and become fabulously wealthy. He searched the vast African continent for years looking for diamonds and finally found himself broke, alone, sick, and thoroughly disgusted. So he threw himself into the ocean and drowned.

Meanwhile, back on the farm he had sold, the new owner was out watering a mule in a stream which ran through the farm. As he looked down into the water he noticed a strange stone that reflected light in an unusual way. He took it back to his house and placed it on a mantelpiece as a curio and thought no more of it.

Some months later the same traveler stopped by the farm. He walked into the house, looked up on the mantelpiece, and exclaimed, "Did the original owner of the farm return?" The new owner replied, "No, he did not." The traveler picked up the stone and said, "This is a diamond of inestimable value," and asked the new owner to show him where he had found it. They went to the stream where the new owner had been watering his mule and as they looked they found another diamond, and another, and another. It turned out that the whole farm was literally covered with acres of diamonds. The old farmer had gone off seeking diamonds somewhere else without looking right under his own backyard.

Many of us are like the old farmer, looking for opportunity when actually many opportunities lie under our own feet. Most of us don't recognize them at first. Diamonds don't look like diamonds in their rough form. At first, they look like rough rocks. They must be cut, shaped, and polished to bring out their best facets. Opportunities are also sometimes disguised as challenges, adversity, and hard work. You must use your talents, abilities and experience to recognize, polish, and shape them. If you fail to look for opportunity you will fail to see it. Learn to identify opportunity and by using your special gifts you may find acres of diamonds in your own backyard.

STEP UP!

The stairs of opportunity
Are sometimes hard to climb;
And that can only be well done
By one step at a time.
But those who would go to the top
Never sit down and despair;
Instead of staring up the steps
One just keeps stepping up the stairs.

KEEP CLIMBING

Life is a struggle, a continual climb, if we're ever to reach our goal;
Requiring real effort from dawn to dusk, or we slip and mar our soul.

For the road of life is rough and rugged, with many a stone in the way; And only with courage and a will to win, can we reach the summit one day.

It was never intended that the going be easy, that our pathway be strewn with flowers;

But by overcoming hardships day by day, we grow stronger in our various powers. Then up with your chin and out with a smile, start pushing your way to the top;

The higher you climb, the better the view; keep right on going, never say stop. There will be many on the road of life, to caution you of the dangers you face. Suggesting you turn back, give up the goal, and with them your footsteps retrace.

Right then is the time to show your courage, and decide for once and for all; That your life's task lies directly ahead, and on this decision, rise or fall.

Then in faith push on to heights sublime, not back to the land of ease; You'll always find light facing sun, and shadows in the rear, if you please.

The higher you climb, the greater the zeal, the more courage you will have if you believe; But you have to call on your ambition and keep climbing, if you ever want to achieve.

Author Unknown

PURPOSE

Just Passing Through

One day a traveler was passing through a country town on his way to a neighboring city. As luck would have it, he accidently turned down a remote road. After traveling several miles trying to find his way back to the highway, he decided to pull into a small country gas station to fill up with fuel.

As the attendant approached his car, the driver called out from his car window. "Friend, I need your help. I'm lost." The station attendant smiled at the traveler and asked, "Do you know where you are?" "I know the name of this town. I saw the sign a few miles back." answered the traveler. "Do you know where you want to go?" asked the attendant. "Yes," the traveler replied, and named his destination. The attendant finished filling the tank and walked up to the car window. Handing the traveler a receipt the station attendant said, "You're not lost son, you just need some directions." He then proceeded to tell the traveler how to get back to the main highway.

As strange as it may seem, very few people really know what they truly want out of life. They are often unsatisfied with things as they are, but when you ask them, specifically, what they want, you'll typically get a vague answer. And since they haven't bothered to determine their true, individual purpose, they drift through life feeling lost and discouraged. Many men and women fail in life, not for lack of ability, or knowledge, or even courage, but simply because they have never organized their energies around a definite purpose. If you were to walk up to the ticket counter at the airport and say, "Give me a ticket," the logical question for the ticket agent to ask would be, "Where are you going?" You would probably feel a little embarrassed starting out on a trip without knowing your destination. And yet, many of us travel through our most important journey—our journey through life, without a clear idea why or where we are going.

Defining your central purpose in life gives you direction. It is a road map consisting of your ambitions, dreams and goals guiding you as you travel through life's journey. Having a clearly defined purpose helps you be enthusiastic about your future. It is your grand mission in life. In helping you define your purpose, ask yourself these questions:

1) *What specifically would I like to have, be, or do in life?* What is that one thing that you can get excited about, that would inspire you to motivate yourself to get up early, work hard all day, and enjoy every minute of your life. 2) *Who am I as a person?* Identify your talents. 3) *What can I contribute to life that would enrich, inspire and empower me and those around me?* What can you contribute to making the world a better place in which to live? 4) *What direction am I taking in life?* Are you heading toward a purpose that will bring you happiness, fulfillment and meaning?

Many people, as author Zig Ziglar wrote, are "wandering generalities" rather than "meaningful specifics." They don't know what they really want out of life.

When you develop a feeling that something is missing in your life never become discouraged. You haven't lost anything, you just need direction. Define what you truly want in life. Then pursue it with confidence and passion.

MY PURPOSE

To waken each morning with a smile brightening my face;
To greet the day with reverence for the opportunities it contains;
To approach my work with a clean mind;
To hold ever before me, even in the doing of little things,
the Ultimate Purpose toward which I am working;
To meet men and women with laughter on my lips and love in my heart;
To be gentle, kind, and courteous through all hours;
To approach the night with weariness that ever woos sleep,
and the joy that comes from work well done—
This is how I desire to spend wisely my days.

THOMAS DEKKER

SUCCESS

Hungry for Success

A foreign exchange student attending school in America, asked his grandfather from eastern Europe to come and visit him. When he arrived, the two spent the next few days touring the college campus. On the day before his grandfather was scheduled to leave, the young student asked his grandfather to meet him after his class at the school cafeteria for lunch.

The grandfather arrived a little early and sat down at an empty table and waited for someone to take his order, but nobody did. Finally, a student with her tray of food sat down opposite him and informed him how the cafeteria worked. "Start out at that end," she said. "Just go along the line and pick out what you want. At the other end they will tell you how much you have to pay."

A few minutes later the young student arrived. Explaining what had happened the grandfather told his grandson, "I have learned how everything works here in America. Life's a cafeteria here. You can get anything you want as long as you are willing to pay the price. You can even get success, but you will never get it if you wait for someone to bring it to you. You have to get up and get it yourself."

What is success to you? It is important to define success as you personally relate to it and what it means to you. For some people, success is spelled $ucce$$. To be successful is often related to having a lot of money or material possessions. You can find many people, however, who have large amounts of money and material wealth who are very unhappy. Is that success? Each one of us has our own definition of what success means to us. Success is personal; it is being involved in something that brings you total happiness and personal satisfaction. Success is achieving whatever you want to achieve. Many people never learn the secret that success is more *who you are* than what you do, and, especially, what you have. No matter what your definition of success is, you must be willing to get out and search for it because no one is going to bring it to you. Success doesn't come to you, you go to it

The other prerequisite for success and one of most importance is that you must be willing to pay the price. Many people succeed because they cheerfully pay the price for success. Others, though they claim to have the ambition and a desire to succeed, are unwilling to pay the price.

What is the price of success? It is having the discipline to concentrate deeply and constantly on your goals while never losing sight or focus. You must develop within yourself a highly sustained determination to achieve what you set out to accomplish despite all the adverse circumstances that may confront you. You must have the self-confidence that there are no obstacles stronger than the belief in your ability to overcome them.

Success is a matter of being able to spend your life in your own way. If you want to be successful at achieving your goals in life, you must ask yourself: "Am I willing to endure the pain of this struggle for the comforts and rewards that go with achievement?" "Or shall I accept the uneasy and inadequate contentment that comes with mediocrity?" "Will I get up and create my own success?" "Am I willing to pay the price for success?"

TEN RULES TO SUCCESS

Work Hard. Hard work is the best investment a person can make.

Study Hard. Knowledge enables a person to work more intelligently and effectively.

Have Initiative. Ruts often deepen into graves.

Love Your Work. Then you will find pleasure in mastering it.

Be Exact. Slipshod methods bring slipshod results.

Have the Spirit of Conquest. Thus you can successfully battle and overcome difficulties.

Cultivate Personality. Personality is to a human what perfume is to the flower.

Help and Share with Others. The real test of business greatness lies in giving opportunity to others.

Be Democratic. Unless you feel right towards your fellow beings you can never be a successful leader.

In All Things Do Your Best. The one who has done his or her best has done everything. The one who has done less than his or her best has done nothing.

CHARLES M. SCHWAB

A SMILE

A smile costs nothing but gives much. It enriches those who receive, without making poorer those who give. It takes but a moment, but the memory of it sometimes lasts forever. No one is so rich or mighty that he can get along without it, and no one is so poor but that he can be made rich by it. A smile creates happiness in the home, fosters good will in business, and is the countersign of friendship. It brings rest to the weary, cheer to the discouraged, sunshine to the sad, and is nature's best antidote for trouble. Yet it cannot be bought, begged, borrowed, or stolen, for it is something that is of no value to anyone until it is given away. Some people are too tired to give a smile. Give them one of yours, as no one needs a smile so much as he who has none to give.

AUTHOR UNKNOWN

UNDERSTANDING

Plain as Black and White

O ne day, an executive called into her office two employees who were having a misunderstanding over a project they were working on. Inside her desk, she pulled out a little two-colored ball. One side of the ball was white, the other, black. Holding the ball between the two employees, she asked, "What color is this little ball?" The person on her left quickly responded, "White."

The other employee who could only see the right side of the ball replied, "Black." As the two employees stared at the ball, from their own angles, they could never agree on the color. The executive then told her confused employees, "Unless you understand each other's point-of-view, there will be no agreement on the color of the ball."

How many disagreements could be quickly resolved if we would take the time to look at both sides of a situation? Developing an awareness of the needs, feelings, problems, and views of others is crucial to successful relationships. Not everyone can see 'eye-to-eye' and we are all entitled to our own point-of-view and perceptions. Recognizing the wants and desires of others helps you improve your understanding of why people act or react as they do toward you or a given situation. Henry Ford shared this insight when he stated, "If there is any secret to success, it lies in the ability to get the other person's point-of-view and see things from his angle as well as from your own." People who are insensitive to the wants and needs of others become inflexible and often convey a 'I win, you lose attitude.' On the other hand, when you develop a clear understanding for others, your personal philosophy becomes 'If I help you win, then I win and we win together.' When you show a sincere interest and understanding in others, they in return will show a sincere interest and understanding in you. Dale Carnegie wrote, "You can make more friends in two months by becoming interested in other people than you can in two years by trying to get other people interested in you."

Underlining this statement is the fact that your success in dealing with others is the result of your efforts to be genuinely interested in people's needs and desires along with understanding what is important to them. Once you've defined this, you have the ability to see a situation as the other side sees it. Understanding simply means communication. Talking, listening, and understanding together go hand-in-hand.

Successful interaction with others does not begin with being understood, but with understanding others. It has been said that when you want to convert someone to your view, you go over to where they are standing, take them by the hand, and guide them. You don't stand across the room and shout at them; you don't call them a dummy; you don't order them to come over to where you are. You start from where they are and work from that position.

Every person has his or her own way of perceiving the world. Even though another person's ideas may seem much different from your own, they may still be enormously useful to you. They may offer another perspective that might never have occurred to you. Learn to share other people's feelings by trying to see things, even if you don't agree with them, from their point-of-view.

IF I KNEW YOU

If I knew you and you knew me;
  if both of us could clearly see,
And with an inner sight divine,
  the meaning of your heart and mine.
I'm sure that we should differ less;
And clasp our hands in friendliness;
Our thoughts would pleasantly agree,
  If I knew you and you knew me.

If I knew you and you knew me,
  as each one knows his ownself,
we could look each other in the face,
  and see therein a truer grace.
Life has so many hidden woes,
So many thorns for every rose,
The "Why" of things our hearts would see
  If I knew you and you knew me.

N. WATERMAN

The aim of life is to live, and to live means to be aware—
joyously, drunkenly,serenely, divinely aware.

HENRY MILLER

Change is the law of life, and those who look only to the past
or the present are certain to miss the future.

JOHN F. KENNEDY

Whenever you face a decision you have three chances:
Do what you please; do what others do; or do what is right.

A. BANNING

See things as you would have them be instead of as they are.

ROBERT COLLIER

We cannot become what we need to be by remaining what we are.

MAX DE PREE

Knowledge is a treasure but practice is the key to it.

The door of opportunity is not locked, not even latched.
Push is the only opener you need—"*push.*"

Purpose is the engine, the power that drives and directs our lives.

J. NOE

Success comes from having a chance or taking a chance.
It comes from improving an opportunity or creating one.

It is better to understand a little than to misunderstand a lot.

CHAPTER 5

THE BEST *of* ALL
POSSIBLE WORLDS

TAKE TIME

Take time to work—it is the price of success.
Take time to think—it is the source of power.
Take time to play—it is the secret of perpetual youth.
Take time to read—it is the foundation of wisdom.
Take time to worship—it is the highway to reverence.
Take time to be friendly—it is the road to happiness.
Take time to dream—it is hitching one's wagon to a star.
Take time to love and be loved—it is the privilege of the gods.
Take time to live—it is one secret of success.
Take time for friendship—it is a source of happiness.
Take time to laugh—it helps lift life's load

ANONYMOUS

EXPERIENCE

Knowing the Ropes

A young woman working for an advertising firm received a promotion to president. She had never dreamed that she would have such an important position. In the history of the firm, all of the past presidents had been older, and had many more years of experience than she did.

The woman approached the venerable Chairman of the Board and said, "I have been appointed president of this advertising firm. I am very honored. I know that I have the knowledge and leadership ability to continue to move us forward in this very competitive business. I come to you today for advice."

Before she was able to ask her question, the chairman responded, "Right decisions!" Puzzled, the young executive said, "That's really helpful, and I appreciate it. Can you be more specific? How do I make right decisions?" The chairman stood up from his chair, walked over to the young woman, and said, "Experience!" The woman responded, "Well, that's the point of my being here today. I feel that I may not have the kind of experience I need. How do I get it?" The serious expression on the chairman's face turned to a smile as he said, "I can answer that in two words, "Wrong decisions!"

Experience is a wonderful thing. It enables us to recognize mistakes that we've made before. It has been said that there is not a man or woman alive who could not retire comfortably in their old age if they could sell their experience for what it cost them. Experience is the great school master of life. Through the lessons of our daily experiences, along with the trials and difficulties we encounter, we gain wisdom and continue to grow. Experience gives us the ability to take the worst and make the best of it. Experience comes from, not only what happens to us, but also what we do with what happens to us. As Winston Churchill stated, "You can tell the character of the person by the choices [decisions] made under pressure."

We all have heard the expressions: "Experience is the best teacher," and "I learned from experience not to ever do that again." Many times what we experience is through the wisdom we gain from the school of hard knocks. As these maxims suggest, we benefit from our experiences of trying or unpleasant situations. A useful axe must be sharp, but to have a sharp axe we must be willing to allow it to suffer loss on the grindstone. In a similar way, we gain understanding and wisdom through the grindstone of experience. Trials and adversity allow us to be "sharpened" through loss, and this enables us to make clearer and better decisions about the future. The decisions we make today, good or bad, will ultimately shape our destiny and the experiences we will encounter along the way.

In the school of experience we get the test first, and then the lesson. None of us learn to make right decisions without being free to make wrong ones. Let your past experiences be your guidepost, not your hitching post. Let your experiences of tomorrow move you closer to success and happiness.

You will learn many lessons.
You are enrolled in a full-time informal school called life. Each day in this school you will have the opportunity to learn lessons. You may like the lessons or think them irrelevant and stupid.

There are no mistakes, only lessons.
Growth is a process of trail and error, and experimentation. The "failed" experiments are as much a part of the process as the experiment that ultimately "works."

A lesson is repeated until learned.
A lesson will be presented to you in various forms until you have learned it. When you have learned it, you can then go on to the next lesson.

Learning lessons does not end.
There is no part of life that does not contain its lessons. If you are alive, there are lessons to be learned.

"There" is no better than "here."
When your "there" has become a "here" you will simply obtain another "there" that will again, look better than "here."

What you make of your life is up to you.
You have all the tools and resources you need. What you do with them is up to you. The choice is yours.

Your answers lie inside you.
The answers to life's questions lie inside you. All you need to do is look, listen and trust.

Anonymous

FAITH

Leap of Faith

Late one afternoon a little girl was playing in her backyard and climbed up an old maple tree. She climbed about halfway to the top. Realizing how far up she had climbed she became frightened. It was starting to get dark outside making it difficult to see. So she began climbing back down and soon found herself stuck in the middle of the tree. The sun had finally set and the little girl was becoming even more frightened. She started to cry, and yelled as loud as she could to her parents.

Her father heard her from inside the house and ran out to the backyard and said, "What's wrong Sharon? Are you all right? Where are you? I can't see you." The little girl cried out, "Daddy, I'm stuck up here in the tree and I can't get down. I'm scared." The father said, "Don't worry I'll get you down." The father walked up to the tree and saw her standing on a branch only a few feet from the ground. The tree was heavily covered with leaves and branches blocking the little girl's vision. The father looked up at his daughter and said, "Jump. Don't be afraid. I'll catch you." The little girl hesitated, "I can't jump, it's too dark and I can't see you. The father answered, "That's all right honey, I can see you."

Faith is a belief or trust that does not question or ask for proof. It is believing in a person, idea, or thing when common sense tells you not to. Faith is the substance of things hoped for, the evidence of things not seen. You must have faith to achieve success—faith in yourself, faith in your ideas, and faith that you will achieve what you have set out to accomplish. Loss of faith causes loss of dreams.

Often times when misfortune strikes we find it difficult to accept. Having the faith that things always work out for the best enables you to stand up against the darkness of doubt and fear. This confident belief gives you courage and strength to do what you must to reach your goals. Building on faith and confidence in yourself and your ability to achieve, allows you to feel unthreatened by setbacks and failure. Without faith in yourself, you would be unwilling to attempt anything or risk doing something which you have never done. With faith you can accomplish what seems to be insurmountable. As poet Walt Whitman wrote, "The steps of faith fall on the seeming void and find the rock beneath." Faith sees the invisible, believes the incredible and receives the impossible. It is the single element that gives you the courage to endure the present as you anticipate the future.

You can overcome doubt and insecurities with faith. Faith in God; faith in yourself; faith in our fellow man. You should omit none of these three from your heart and mind. Without faith in God, there is no hope for the soul; without faith in yourself, life is full of trials and defeats; without faith in each other, we miss the trust and joys of friendship.

Keep your faith bright, let its luster never grow dim. If you have faith, nothing shall be impossible unto you. Have the faith to step out on the branch of uncertainty, then jump and grab hold of the great opportunities that lie before you.

HAVE FAITH

The more faith you have
The more you believe,
The more goals you set
The more you'll achieve.

So reach for the stars
Pick a mountain to climb,
Dare to think big
But give yourself time.

Remember no matter
How futile things seem,
With faith, there is no
Impossible Dream!

AUTHOR UNKNOWN

FORGIVENESS

Sweet Forgiveness

A boy attending summer camp received a package in the mail from his mother. She had baked him a dozen of his favorite cookies. He ate a few, and then placed the remainder under his bunk. When he returned to his cabin later that day to get another cookie, the box was gone.

That afternoon a camp counselor, who had been told of the misfortune, saw another boy behind a tree eating the missing cookies. Wanting to teach him that it is wrong to take something that didn't belong to him, the counselor sought out the boy whose cookies had been taken. He said, "Johnny, I know who took your cookies. Will you help me teach him a lesson?" The puzzled boy replied, "Well, yes— but aren't you going to punish him?" The counselor explained, "If I punish him, he will become resentful and hate you. I want you to call your mother and ask her to send you another box of cookies." The boy complied.

When the second box of cookies arrived, the counselor said, "Now, the boy who took your cookies is down by the lake. Go down there and share your cookies with him." Johnny protested, "But he was wrong in what he did!" "I know," the counselor replied, "but try it and see what happens."

Soon the camp counselor saw the two boys coming up the hill, arm and arm. The boy who had taken the cookies was earnestly trying to get Johnny to accept his pocket knife in payment for the stolen cookies, and Johnny was just as earnestly refusing the gift from his new friend. That day the two boys learned a valuable lesson, one they found to be much more satisfying than a few cookies. It is the sweet lesson of forgiveness.

Forgive and forget remain two of the most important words ever spoken. When we forgive, we in no way change the past, but we most certainly change the future, our future of happiness. Napoleon wrote, "One must learn to forgive and not hold a hostile, bitter attitude of mind, which offends those about us and prevents us from enjoying ourselves; one must recognize human shortcomings and adjust himself to them rather than to be constantly finding fault with them."

The power of complete forgiveness enables us to let go of negative feelings and free ourselves from anger, resentment, misery and bitterness. Holding on to negative feelings toward someone robs us of energy. When we are unforgiving toward someone, we give them power over us. We give them the power to influence our feelings in a hurtful way, even though the incident may have occurred long ago. When we forgive someone for their negative behavior we're giving them the opportunity to do better. By forgiving someone who has wronged us, thus releasing our hostility and hatred, we improve our mental and physical health.

Begin today with a clean slate. Write out a forgiveness list. Forgive someone who has caused you hurt. Forgive and forget the negative events of the past. Forgive yourself for your shortcomings. One of the secrets of a long and happier life is to forgive everybody and everything each night before you go to bed. Allow yourself peace of mind by letting go of any injustices you feel that others have done you.

Acknowledge the hurt. This step is not as natural as it might seem. Actually, it may entail swallowing your pride and admitting that you are not as impervious to deep hurt as you thought.

Decide to forgive. You can make this decision even before you know whether forgiveness is possible or how it can be achieved.

Understand that forgiveness isn't easy. If the prospect or retribution has been a burning, consuming force in your life, you may experience a profound void (as if a part of you is gone) after deciding to forgive.

Forgive yourself. In most human conflicts mistakes are made on both sides. Being willing to forgive yourself for your negligence or excesses will make it easier to extend forgiveness to the other party.

Remember the consequences of not forgiving. A proverb aptly describes the outcome of non-forgiveness: "He that cannot forgive others breaks the bridge over which he must pass himself; for every man has need to be forgiven."

D. DONNELLY

TRUE FRIENDSHIP

True friendship is a harmony between souls rather than between minds. Our best friends are those with whom we are most in unison at heart. It is not needful that friends always think alike. Often they hold opinions as far apart as the poles, but there must be a unity of spirit and a mutual heart throb if friendship is to be of the enduring kind. When two people hold this relation to each other, they are more than mere acquaintances—they are friends.

M. PETERSON

FRIENDSHIP

Rocky Roads and Smooth Friendships

A little girl was riding her bike through the park one day and stopped in front of a very large rock in the middle of her path. She got off her bike and tried to lift it but it was too large for someone her size. She pushed, pulled, and even kicked it as she tried in vain to lift the huge stone. In spite of her efforts the rock would not budge. A boy riding by on his bike noticed the girl struggling and asked her if she was having trouble. "I have tried everything and it won't move!" answered the girl. "Are you using all your strength?" the boy asked. Exasperated the girl replied, "Yes, I am." The boy asked, "Have you looked around the park and tried to use everything at your disposal?" The girl looked up, frustration filling her face, and shouted, "Yes!" The boy then got off his bike walked over to the girl and said softly, "No you haven't. You haven't asked for my help."

To be a source of strength and comfort for those who are faced with difficulty is to be a true friend. A friend is someone who is always there to help when you need it most. As the popular song states, "We get by with a little help from our friends." Developing lasting friendship is based on your commitment to helping others fulfill their desires without expecting anything in return. To be a friend you should strive to lift people up, not cast them down. You should encourage, not discourage. You should set an example that will be an inspiration to others. A friend is someone who is tolerant; has an understanding heart and a forgiving nature. A true friend is someone you can share your hopes, aspirations, and deepest secrets with. A friend is someone to whom you can take your joy or sorrow and who is willing to share it with you. A friend will celebrate with you in your victories or pick you up and brush you off if you stumble and fall. A friend focuses on your positive aspects instead of pointing to your faults and weaknesses. A friend is a good listener, is one who offers advice without criticizing, and is loyal and trustworthy. Friendship radiates love.

As you can see a true friend is a priceless gift. Today, do something for a friend that expresses your gratitude that he or she is your friend. Let your friends know just how much you appreciate them.

WHAT IS A FRIEND

A friend is someone who is concerned with everything you do.
A friend is someone to call upon during good and bad times.
A friend is someone who understands whatever you do.
A friend is someone who tells you the truth about yourself.
A friend is someone who knows what you are going through at all times.
A friend is someone who does not compete with you.
A friend is someone who is genuinely happy for you when things go well.
A friend is someone who tries to cheer you up when things don't go well.
A friend is an extension of yourself without which you are not complete.

SUSAN POLIS SCHUTZ

IF NOBODY CARED

If nobody smiled and nobody cheered and nobody helped us along,
If every last one just looked after himself and the good things all
    went to the strong;
If nobody cared just a little for you, and nobody thought about me,
And we stood alone in the battle of life,
    what a dreary old world this would be.
Life is sweet just because friends we have made,
And the things which in common we share.
We want to live on, not because of ourselves,
But because of the people who care.
It's the giving and doing for somebody else—
On that all life's splendor depends,
And the joy of the world, when you've summed it all up,
Is found in the making of friends.

Author Unknown

GIVING

The Gift from Within

A wanderer who was traveling in the mountains found a precious stone in a stream. The next day he met another traveler who was hungry, and the wanderer opened his bag to share his food. The hungry traveler saw the precious stone in the wanderer's bag, admired it, and asked the wanderer to give it to him. The wanderer did so without hesitation. The traveler left, rejoicing in his good fortune. He knew the jewel was worth enough to give him security for the rest of his life.

But a few days later he came back searching for the wanderer. When he found him, he returned the stone and said, "I have been thinking. I know how valuable this stone is, but I give it back to you in the hope that you can give me something much more precious. If you can, give me what you have within you that enabled you to give me the stone."

It has been said that you give but little when you give of your possessions. It is when you give of yourself that you truly give. Emerson gave us true insight when he wrote, "Rings and jewels are not gifts, but apologies for gifts. The only true gift is a portion of thyself." When you give to the world the best you have, the best will come back to you. Begin today by giving away the best of yourself. Give someone your time, your attention, your wisdom. Give away your positive attitude, courtesy, and appreciation. Give away gifts from the heart: love, kindness, joy, understanding, sympathy, tolerance and forgiveness. Give away your gifts of the mind: ideas, dreams, and talents. Give gifts of the spirit: prayer, vision, peace, and faith. Give the gift of kind words: encouragement, inspiration, and guidance. Give away a skill or ability that will help others. When you give out of the fullness of your heart you feel good about yourself and it will help build your self-esteem. The are many ways that you can give of yourself through random acts of kindness each day: smiling at others as they pass you, a compliment or kind word. Remember that what you keep to yourself, you lose; what you give away, you keep forever. Give the gift of giving yourself away to others.

LIVING AND GIVING

Whatever you give away today, or think or say or do, will multiply ten fold then return to you. It may not come immediately nor from the obvious source, but the law applies unfailingly through some invisible force. Whatever you feel about another, be it love or hate or passion, will surely bounce right back at you in some clear or secret fashion. If you speak about some person, a word of praise or two, soon tens of people will speak it back to you. Our thoughts are broadcasts of the soul, not secrets of the brain. Kind ones bring us happiness, petty ones untold pain. Giving works as surely as reflections in a mirror. If hate you sent, hate you will get back, but loving brings love nearer. Remember as you start this day and duty crowds your mind, that kindness comes so quickly back to those who first are kind. Let that thought and this one direct you through each day. The only things we ever keep are the things we give away.

JERRY BUCHANAN

GIVING AND RECEIVING

I launched a smile; far out it sailed
    On life's wide troubled sea.
And many more than I could count
    Came sailing back to me.

I clasped a hand while whispering,
    "The clouds will melt away."
I felt my life was very blessed
All through the hours that day.

I sent a thought of happiness
    Where it was needed sore,
And very soon thereafter, found
    Joy adding to my store.

I wisely shared my slender hoard,
    Toil-earned coins of gold;
But soon it flowed right back,
    Increased a hundredfold.

I helped another climb a hill,
    A little thing to do;
And yet it brought a rich reward,
    A friendship that was new.

I think each morning when I rise,
    Of how I may achieve,
I know by serving I advance,
    By giving I receive.

THOMAS GAINES

HAPPINESS

The Hidden Secret

According to a legend told by the ancient Greeks, the gods on Mount Olympus held a council to decide where they could hide the secret to happiness so that when it was found, the people would appreciate it more. "Let us hide it on the highest mountain. It will never be found there," one god replied. "Let us bury it deep into the earth," another suggested. Still others suggested that the secret to happiness be buried in the dark depths of the deepest ocean. Finally, one of the gods came up with a solution. "Let us hide the secret to happiness in the last place that anyone would ever look, a place they will only come to when all other possibilities are exhausted." He continued, "We will hide the secret to happiness deep within the people themselves."

For thousands of years, men and women have searched for the secret that would enable them to live a more happy and successful life. To this day, many people continue to look for this hidden secret, seldom ever finding its hiding place. Most of us never realize that it lies deep within each of us.

Abraham Lincoln stated, "Most people are about as happy as they make up their mind to be." Happiness is basically determined by the attitude you hold toward yourself and the world in which you live. As someone once stated, "The city of happiness can be found in the *state of mind*." Happiness does not depend upon a full pocketbook, but upon a mind full of rich thoughts and a heart full of rich emotions. No matter what your definition of happiness may be, and each of us has our own personal feeling of what truly makes us happy in our own life, you may follow the insight offered by John D. Rockefeller as he stated, "The road to happiness lies in two simple principles; find what it is that interests you and that you can do well, and when you find it put your whole soul into it—every bit of energy and ambition and natural ability you have."

The basis for happiness can be found in something to do, something to love, and something to look forward to. Lasting happiness comes from putting your heart into that which you enjoy doing and working at it with joy and enthusiasm. Happiness also grows out of harmonious relationships with others based on attitudes of good will, tolerance, understanding, and love.

A cheerful heart is one which grows larger by helping others. This philosophy of happiness is pointedly expressed in the old Hindu proverb, which states: "Help thy brother's boat across, and lo! thine own has reached the shore."

Happiness is not given to you; it can only be experienced within. How do you define the word <u>happiness</u>? If you were asked to fill in the blank after the question, "I would be perfectly happy if...," how would you answer? The Greek philosopher Aristotle once wrote, "The single most common denominator of mankind is the desire to be happy, however happiness may be defined by the individual."

Deciding exactly what it is that will bring you joy and peace of mind is the starting point to achieving happiness in your life. Through this self-discovery you will uncover the secret and the hiding place of happiness. It's not far. It can be found buried deep within your own heart and soul.

THINKING HAPPINESS

Think of the things that make you happy,
Not the things that make you sad;
Think of the fine and true in mankind,
Not its sordid side and bad;
Think of the blessings that surround you,
Not the ones that are denied;
Think of the virtues of your friendships,
Not the weak and faulty side;

Think of the gains you've made in business,
Not the losses you've incurred;
Think of the good of you that is spoken,
Not some cruel, hostile word;
Think of the days of health and pleasure,
Not the days of woe and pain;
Think of the days alive with sunshine,
Not the dismal days of rain;

Think of the hopes that lie before you,
Not the waste that lies behind;
Think of the treasures you have gathered,
Not the ones you've failed to find;
Think of the service you may render,
Not of serving self alone;
Think of the happiness of others,
And in this you'll find your own!

ROBERT E. FARLEY

INVOCATION OF THE DAWN

Look to this day!
For it is life, the very life of life.
In its brief course lie all the verities
All the realities of existence;
The bliss of growth,
The glory of action,
The splendor of beauty;

For yesterday is already a dream,
And tomorrow is only a vision;
But today, well-lived,
Makes every yesterday a dream of happiness
And every tomorrow a vision of hope.
Look well, therefore, to this day!

ANONYMOUS

HOPE

The Light That Never Grew Dim

L ong ago, in the days of sailing ships, a terrible storm arose and a ship was lost in a deserted area. Only one crewman survived, washed up on a small uninhabited island. Each day he looked for a passing ship but saw nothing. Eventually he managed to build a crude hut, in which he stored the few things he had recovered from the wreck and those things he had made to help him. One day, as the sailor was returning from his daily search for food, he saw a large column of smoke. As he ran toward it, he saw his small hut in flames. All was lost.

Although slightly stunned, he quickly began to search the island for material to build a new hut. That night, he worked diligently to construct a better dwelling than that which he had before, and he remained hopeful that one day he would finally be discovered. He spent an almost sleepless night thinking of constructive ways in which to make his time on the island more comfortable. The next morning, he rose early and went down to the sea. There, to his amazement, he saw a ship lying offshore and a small boat rowing toward him. When the once-marooned man met the ship's captain, he asked him how he had known to send help. The captain replied, "Why, we saw your smoke signal yesterday, but by the time we drew close the tide was against us, so we had to wait until now to come and get you."

Hope is that single ingredient which allows us to look forward to tomorrow and the positive opportunities it will bring. Hope is the energy that arouses the mind to explore every possibility in time of challenges and adversity. Hope is that extra push that keeps us going. It gives us the ability to carry on with our plans even though we feel discouraged or doubtful. Sometimes it may seem that things have taken a turn for the worst, but the hopeful heart believes that, "Better times are just around the corner."

When failure confronts you, when disappointment faces you, when disaster threatens you, the only hope you have is hope. For as long as you have hope, you will always feel a candle burning within you that will light the way to great possibilities.

HOPE IN ACTION

Hope opens doors where despair closes them.
Hope discovers what can be done instead of grumbling about what cannot.
Hope draws its power from a deep trust in God and the basic goodness of mankind.
Hope "lights a candle" instead of "cursing the darkness."
Hope regards problems, small or large, as opportunities.
Hope sets big goals and is not frustrated by repeated difficulties or setbacks.
Hope pushes ahead when it would be easy to quit.
Hope puts up with modest gains, realizing that "the longest journey starts with one step."
Hope accepts misunderstandings as the price for serving the greater good of others.
Hope is a good loser, because it has the divine assurance of final victory.

R. ARMSTRONG

IT MIGHT HAVE BEEN WORSE

Sometimes I pause and sadly think
Of the things that might have been,
Of the golden chances I let slip by,
And which never returned again.

I think of the joys that might have been mine:
The prizes I almost won,
The goals I missed by a mere hair's breathe
And the things I might have done.

It fills me with gloom when I ponder this,
Till I look on the other side,
How I might have been completely engulfed
By misfortune's surging tide.

The unknown dangers lurking about—
Which I passed safely through
The evils and sorrows that I've been spared
Pass plainly now in review.

So when I am downcast and feeling sad,
I repeat over and over again,
Things are far from being as bad
As they easily might have been.

G.T. RUSSELL

KINDNESS

Begging for Kindness

A very wealthy lady of high rank decided on a miserably cold day to test the kindheartedness and goodwill of her neighbors. She put on some ragged clothes, covered her head with a shawl, and went on her way in her convincing disguise carrying an old woven basket. At some houses she was given things of absolutely no value; at others she was spurned with harsh words. Only at one home was she received with kindness, and that was at the home of a poor man. Here, she was taken into a warm room and fed a warm meal.

The next day all the people the lady had visited were unexpectedly invited to her estate, where they were led by servants to a spacious dining room. Place cards showed each guest where to sit at the table. On the plate before each person was the same thing that person had given the disguised lady the day before. Many plates were completely empty. Only the poor man was served a heaping plate of appetizing food. Then the wealthy lady entered the dining room and explained to the guests, "Yesterday, to test your kindheartedness, I went about the neighborhood dressed as a beggar. Today I am serving you the same thing you gave me."

Wouldn't it be a different world if we could learn to become more caring and more unselfish. If someone were to pay you ten cents for every kind word or act that you said or did and collect five cents for every unkind word or act, would you be rich or poor? Sharing kindness with others is the most rewarding and fulfilling act you can do.

Kindness is always returned to the one who sends it out. You reap just what you sow. What you do to and for others tends to come back to you. It has been said that kindness is a hard thing to give away because it keeps coming back to the giver. By helping other people and by doing kind things for them, you will experience an inward satisfaction and joy that is immeasurable.

There is nothing more comforting, more gratifying than knowing that through a kind word or act you made someone else's day a little brighter or someone else's life a little easier. A kind and generous act will go further, last longer, and be remembered long after the prism of politeness or the complexion of courtesy has faded away. Can you think of a kind word or deed that you could do for someone that would put a smile on their face and in their heart? Give away a random act of kindness to a friend, spouse, co-worker, or to someone you don't know. Today, light up someone's heart with a simple act of kindness. A candle loses nothing of its light by lighting another candle.

GOLDEN RULES

Do all the good you can
By all the means you can
In all the ways you can
In all the places you can
At all times you can
To all the people you can
As long as you can.

ANONYMOUS

CONSIDER

Is anybody happier
Because you passed their way?
Does anyone remember
That you spoke to them today?
This day is almost over,
And its toiling time is through;
Is there anyone to utter now,
A friendly word for you?

Can you say tonight in passing,
With the day that slipped so fast,
That you helped a single person,
Of the many that you passed?
Is a single heart rejoicing,
Over what you did or said?
Does one whose hopes were fading
Now with courage look ahead?

Did you waste the day, or lose it?
Was it well or poorly spent?
Did you leave a trail of kindness,
Or a scar of discontent?

AUTHOR UNKNOWN

LIFE

Faithful Journey

I magine for a moment that you have been sent on a journey. You had no choice about when or where it started. You have no idea when, where or how it will end. You were given no map, and all you do know is that it is going to end sometime. There are certain rules that apply to this journey, but you will have to learn them as you go. There will be certain circumstances which you will have to confront during the journey but you cannot control them. You may not even know the purpose of the journey, even though others may tell you that they know. All you know is that once started, you must continue every day, whether you feel like it or not.

You start with no possessions, and when you finish you must turn in all you have accumulated. At the end of the journey, some say, you will either be rewarded or punished. Would you be enthusiastic about taking a journey with so many unanswered questions and possible outcomes? Well, the journey has already begun, and it's called the journey through life.

Much has been written about this wonderful journey called life, but no one but you can write about your life. You are unique, and so is your life. Consider for a moment that your life is likened to that of a book. You as the author are continually writing and adding new pages and chapters to this book. Not only are you the author but you are also the editor, proof reader, and above all, the main character of the story. And as you reach the final chapter of the book, you alone determine whether or not it was a best seller. You haven't always been the author of this potentially great story. While growing up, many people contributed to its pages. Your parents, teachers, friends, have all in some way coauthored your book of life though their attitudes, beliefs, values, and perceptions. All of your experiences up to this moment, positive or negative, have also contributed in some way to your life story. But now you are taking charge of writing the story line and you control what gets written into the pages. Also as editor, you can identify and evaluate those things that are not in harmony with the type of life you wish to live today.

Looking over all of the pages thus far in your "Life Book," what should the title be? Maybe a few of these titles should be considered: (1) Life...a wonderful fairy tale. (2) Life...a great tragedy. (3) Life... a great adventure. (4) Life...an endless soap opera. (5) Life...a love story. (6) Life...a story of heartache and pain. (7) Life...a story of great achievement. (8) Life...a story of underachievement.

How you feel about your life right now is an important key to working toward making positive changes. Maybe everything in your life is running smoothly and it suits you very well exactly as it is. However, if you feel that things could be much better and your particular lifestyle is holding you back from happiness and success, then it's up to you to begin rewriting the story line. You cannot go back and change the events of the past, but you can start today to choose how the events of each new day will play a role in your future. Live each day with passion, peace of mind, happiness, and fulfillment. Take your "Life Book" into your hands and continue to add positive experiences to its pages. Live each day by the title: My Life Journey...a best seller!

SAY YES TO LIFE

Say "Yes" to life with a positive constructive attitude.

Say "Yes" with enthusiasm to an interest in other people, in other departments of your company, in your customers and suppliers, in what is going on in your city, state, and nation, and in other nations.

Enthusiasm for life will bring a radiance to your face and voice. People are attracted by the contagious joy that fills you with laughter, that inspires you and those you touch to greater achievement of your own true potential.

Say "Yes" to beauty; the beauty of sunrise and sunset; of a star-filled sky and the wonder of its endlessness; the beauty of flowers, of a child's smile; the beauty of poetry, prose and music. There is so much beauty all around you, take time to see it, hear it, smell it, and be comforted by it! The world isn't drab—appreciate its marvelous colors, sounds, and fragrances.

Say "Yes" to truth. It is often difficult to sort out fact from fiction and come to a valid conclusion. It is perhaps more difficult and courageous to speak the truth. But to do so stamps you as a person of sincerity, genuineness, and honesty. Pursue the truth that makes you free.

Say "Yes" to opportunity. Regardless of financial conditions, the unemployment situation, age or education, there are greater opportunities today than ever in the world's history. It takes alertness to recognize opportunity, work to qualify, and courage to embrace it. Never hesitate because you haven't done the work before, or think you don't measure up. You are far, far greater than you have demonstrated. Say "I can" and go on to the greater unfoldment of your mind and spirit.

Say "Yes" to love. Love is kind, thinks no evil, and rejoices in the truth. Love undergirds you with faith and hope. It helps you to develop the perfection which is your inborn heritage. Say "Yes" to the immense good in life and you will find so great a blessing that there shall not be room enough to receive it.

PAUL POULSEN

YOU MAY COUNT THAT DAY

If you sit down at the set of sun
And count the acts that you have done,
And, counting, find
One self-denying deed, one word
That eased the heart of him who heard—
One glance most kind
That fell like sunshine where it went—
Then you may count that day well spent.

But if, through all the livelong day,
You've cheered no heart, by yea or nay—
If, through it all
You've done nothing that you can trace
That brought the sunshine to one face—
No act most small
That helped some soul and nothing cost—
Then count that day as worse than lost.

GEORGE ELIOT

LOVE

Echo of Love

A little boy shouted to his mother, in an outburst of temper, that he hated her. Fearing punishment, he quickly fled to a nearby hillside. As he sat on a rock overlooking the valley, he released his anger by shouting, "I hate you! I hate you!" Unexpectedly, back from the valley came a loud echo, "I hate you! I hate you!" Startled by the response, the little boy ran back home and told his mother that up in the valley there was a mean little boy shouting that he hated him. His mother walked with him back to the hillside and told him to shout into the valley, "I love you! I love you!" This time the little boy discovered to his surprise that there was another boy in the valley saying, "I love you! I love you!" He turned to his mother and said, "I love you mom." As they walked down the hillside, they could hear the continuing echo, "I love you mom, I love you mom," all the way back home.

The most important and wonderful thing in life is love. Every one of us has an inner desire and overriding need for love. Of all the human abilities, love is by far the most powerful. Love however, means more than receiving the care and concern of others. It also means giving of yourself to others. When you give unconditional love to another, you do so in hope that your love will be accepted and returned in equal measure. The most important thing about love to remember is that you cannot receive it unless you are first willing to give it. Love echoes in the hearts of those who are willing to give of themselves first. Love is the reflection of your deepest feelings; kindness, consideration, gentleness, indulgence, tenderness, unselfishness, and compassion toward others. Only when we experience love in this way can we experience life to the fullest.

Shakespeare wrote, "The fragrance of the rose lingers on the hand that casts it." Whenever you express love and give love to others, it will eventually come back to you. Loving others is a key to life, but you can't love others unless you love yourself. You can't give away what you don't have. In the Bible it is written, "Love your neighbor as much as you love yourself." When you feel good about yourself coupled with a knowledge of self-worth, then it is easy to give love to others. Happiness and success means living a life filled with love, loving everyone unconditionally. There is no real happiness where there is an absence of love.

Here is a simple love potion that will bring you an abundance of joy and happiness, without medicine, without herbs, without any witch's magic. It is simply this: *If you want to be loved then love.*

LOVE IS...

Slow to suspect—quick to trust,
Slow to condemn—quick to justify,
Slow to offend—quick to defend,
Slow to expose—quick to shield,
Slow to reprimand—quick to forbear,
Slow to belittle—quick to appreciate,
Slow to demand—quick to give,
Slow to provoke—quick to help,
Slow to resent—quick to forgive.

THE ART OF LOVE

The spectrum of love merges and focuses all of the arts of living.
Friendship, awareness, happiness, all of the arts of the good life, are
brilliant beads strung on the golden cord of love.

Love is the foundation and the apex of the pyramid of our existence.

Love is the "affirmative of affirmatives"; it enlarges the vision,
expands the heart.

Love is the dynamic motivation behind every worthy purpose; it is
the upward thrust that lifts us to the heights.

Love is the creative fire, the inspiration that keeps the torch of
progress aflame.

Love penetrates the mysteries of life. "Anything," said George
Washington Carver, "will give up its secrets if you love it enough."

Love is the dove of peace, the spirit of brotherhood; it is tenderness
and compassion, forgiveness and tolerance.

Love is the supreme good; it is the overflowing life, the giving of
ourselves to noble ends and causes.

Love is down to earth and it reaches to the highest star; it is the
valley of humility and the mountaintop of ecstasy.

Love is the spiritual magnetism that draws people together for the
working of miracles.

Love is the perfect antidote that floods the mind to wash away hatred,
jealousy, resentment and fear.

Love, is the shining commandment: Love one another.

Love bears with all things, believes all things, hopes all things,
endures all things.

The art of love is God at work through you.

W. A. PETERSON

OPTIMISM

Squeaky Clean Outlook

A man and his wife on a long trip pulled off the road into a full-service gas station. After the station attendant had washed their car's windshield, the man in the car shouted to the station attendant, "It's still dirty. Wash it again." So the station attendant complied. After he finished washing it again and started to hand the man his receipt, the man in the car angrily said, "It's still dirty. Don't you know how to wash a windshield?" Just then the man's wife reached over, removed her husband's glasses from his face, and cleaned them with a tissue. She then placed them back on her husband and behold— the windshield was clean!

What do you see when you look out of your window on the world? Do you see the proverbial glass as half full or half empty? When setbacks knock you down, do you get back up, or do you start thinking about failure? Do you start the morning with a sour outlook toward the coming day— the kind of outlook that dreads the new dawning, or do you tell yourself that this is a great day, the best day of them all? The world can appear pretty grim when our mental disposition is covered with fear, uncertainty, and pessimistic thinking. Our outlook toward the people and experiences we encounter each day can determine the outcome, either positive or negative. When your outlook and expectations are of failure and unhappiness, that's what you will experience. When you adopt an optimistic outlook that a better life is possible, and that things will work out for the best in the end, you have a better chance of bringing positive solutions into a reality. Optimists see problems as solvable instead of impossible, goals as attainable instead of unreachable, and see their abilities as expandable instead of limited. Optimists are joyful, enthusiastic, and excited about life. They tend to take a more hopeful and positive view of life, regardless of the circumstances that may confront them, while pessimists tend to expect the worst.

Many consider an optimist to be a Pollyanna, someone who is out of touch with reality. This statement is far from being true. An optimist recognizes that we live in an imperfect world but does not allow the small percentage of those things that may not be going right in his or her life to affect the larger percentage of those things that are going well. An optimist accepts personal setbacks, tragedies, and obstacles as lessons from which to learn, and as challenges to be mastered.

Optimism offers innumerable benefits toward one's mental and physical heath, longevity, professional and personal success, and overall well-being. You are a living magnet, constantly drawing to your life those things, people, and circumstances in harmony with the thoughts that occupy your mind. If you fill your mind with pessimistic thoughts you, in turn, will draw negative events into your life. If you have negative expectations about your ability to accomplish a task, then it is certain that you won't. On the contrary, if you fill your mind with positive thought and expectations, you will experience positive events in your life. Both work with astounding accuracy.

Adopt the attitude that something wonderful is going to happen to you today, and then go out and discover what it is.

THE OPTIMIST VS. THE PESSIMIST

The optimist turns the impossible into the possible;
the pessimist turns the possible into the impossible.
The optimist pleasantly ponders how high the kite will fly;
the pessimist woefully wonders how soon the kite will fall.
The optimist sees a green near every sand trap;
the pessimist sees a sand trap near every green.
The optimist looks at the horizon and sees an opportunity;
the pessimist peers into the distance and fears a problem.
To the optimist all doors have handles and hinges;
to the pessimist all doors have locks and latches.
The optimist promotes progress, prosperity and plenty;
the pessimist preaches limitations, liabilities and losses.
The optimist accentuates assets, abundance, and advantages;
the pessimist majors in mistakes, misfortunes and misery.
The optimist goes out and finds the bell;
the pessimist gives up and wrings his hands.

WILLIAM ARTHUR WARD

POSITIVE THINKING

Sour Headlines

A businessman was walking to work downtown in a big city and decided to stop off at his regular newspaper stand to buy a paper. He greeted the vendor very courteously, but in return he received abrupt and discourteous service. The vendor had a very sour disposition. Accepting the newspaper, which was rudely shoved in his face, the businessman politely smiled and wished the vendor a nice weekend.

As he walked away, a bystander who had observed all of this walked up to the businessman and asked, "Does he always treat you so rudely?" "Yes, unfortunately he does," answered the businessman. "And are you always so polite and friendly to him?" asked the bystander. "Yes, I am," said the businessman. "Why are you so nice to him when he is so rude to you?" the bystander questioned. The businessman smiled and then replied, "Unfortunately that man has a negative attitude, but I do not. I have no intention of permitting him to give me one. To permit him to annoy me would be to permit him to ruin my day. I have no intention of doing that. If he wants to be unhappy, that's his decision and only he can decide to change it. But one thing is for sure and that is, I'm not going to let him decide how I'm going to feel or act!"

Positive thinking is a way of life rather than a momentary thought. It is an ingrained habit rather than an occasional way of thinking whenever we feel down or depressed or when it looks like things may not be going as we want. Being a positive thinker is the ability to have a positive outlook on life. This in turn promotes positive patterns of thought and actions that make you feel better, think better, and perform better. Positive thinking is a much healthier state of mind than the draining powers of negative thinking. People who have a positive view of life see the world as a good place. They actively seek out the good in other people and situations. Positive thinkers are simply people who have learned how to discipline their attitudes of mind to their advantage. It is an acquired mental skill. As Emerson wrote, "The measure of mental health is the disposition to find good everywhere." In other words, happiness isn't something that comes to you by chance, it comes to you by choice.

What happens if you start your day with a positive disposition and you are confronted with a negative experience as the businessman encountered with the newspaper vendor? Well, this is one of the most important qualities of a positive thinker—*they do not allow external forces to determine how they feel.*

Positive thinkers understand that they have a choice on how to react to a given situation and that choice is theirs. Their attitude and frame of mind is something over which they alone have complete control, not anyone or anything else. They understand that it is not the events that happen in their life, but rather how they react to the events. Positive thinking can also be defined as the "*I can*" opposed to the "*I can't*" way of thinking. It is believing in your possibilities and disbelieving in your doubts.

Positive thinking is not an excuse or cop-out to avoid reality. It doesn't mean you deny the existence of obstacles in your life, but that you expect to master those obstacles. Develop the habit of positive thinking, and you will in turn keep in proper perspective the pessimism so prevalent in our society.

P.M.A. HOW TO MAINTAIN
A POSITIVE MENTAL ATTITUDE

The positive thinker has mental images of optimism, hope and growth
through these ways:

Maintain a spirit of ambition. We have more strength and power than
most of us ever realize.

Remember that seldom is anything you encounter really impossible.
Break it down and analyze its possible solutions.

Do not let anything "get you down." Overcome frustrations and irritations
before they grow into big issues.

Keep yourself feeling young in spirit with enthusiasm.

Don't let yourself slip into tiredness.

Do things for others to give yourself a good feeling through caring and
goodwill.

Have trust and belief in yourself with spiritual commitment.

Never give up. Reevaluate your means toward your goals and maintain
persistence and perseverance.

When confronted with an upsetting situation, remind yourself of your
belief in yourself to increase your courage.

When grief comes, remember you or the person affected needs to be
surrounded with genuine love.

Remember that everyone is confronted with situations that require coping,
confronting, and dealing with them positively.

You have more energy and capacity for vitality in your thinking than
you might realize—start using it and surprise yourself.

Having a deep faith can win over all difficulties.

Finding excitement helps keep a positive mental attitude.

WINNING

Portrait of a Better You

Hoping to find a few days work, a traveling portrait painter stopped at a small town. One of his clients was a man who, despite his dirty, unshaven face and wrinkled clothes, sat for his portrait. As the artist began brushing the canvas, the man began to tell him about how depressed he was. He felt that everything in his life was going wrong, and that nothing ever went his way.

He told the artist that he had lost his job and was having trouble finding work, that he had few friends, and felt as if he were a complete failure. He told the painter that he was giving up hope that things would get any better for him. After listening to the man's hardship story and laboring a little longer than usual, the artist lifted the painting from the easel and presented it to the man. "This isn't me," the man shouted as he studied the smiling, well-dressed man in the painting. The artist, who had looked beyond the exterior and hardship that the man was currently facing replied, "*But it's the man you could become.*"

The painter in this story took to heart the message the German poet Goethe was trying to convey when he wrote, "If I treat you as if you were what you could be, that is what you will become." To feel like a winner you must first see yourself as a winner. Develop winning habits, and you will do the things that winners do. You are an extraordinary human being with natural talents and abilities that will enable you to have and accomplish things you may never have felt possible. Of all the billions of people on earth, and all those who have ever lived, there never has been, nor will there ever be, anyone just like you.

The odds are astronomic that a person will ever be born with your unique combination of characteristics and qualities. If someone were to build a computer to equal the capacity of your mind it would cost billions of dollars and it would still not be complete. Today the estimated cost of the two hundred parts of the anatomy now available artificially comes to about five million dollars. With all this special equipment, you have the potential to do something extraordinary with your life, something no one else can do. To live the winning life you desire and deserve, you must recognize your potential and cultivate the habits of a winner.

Successful people have distinguishing characteristics that allow them to utilize their talents and abilities to become the winners they are capable of becoming. These characteristics include: Contagious enthusiasm, they're fun to be around; they radiate a positive mental attitude; they have self-confidence and believe in themselves; they focus on their strengths, not their weaknesses; they strive for excellence, not perfection; they're persistent achievers; they willingly share their time and their talent; they are self-disciplined; they carry on with their desires in spite of opposition or failure; they recognize that every failure brings with it the seed of an equivalent advantage; they have an invigorating determination to achieve their goals.

Winning is assessed simply by how you feel about life, and how you feel about life is determined by what your life is about. Ask yourself, "Do I currently practice these common characteristics of a winner in my life? Is this me?" Don't worry if you answered no, because *it's the person you could become.*

I AM A WINNER

...because I think like a winner, prepare like a winner, and perform like a winner.

...because I set high but attainable goals, work toward those goals with determination and persistence, and never stop until I reach them.

...because I am strong enough to say "No!" to those things that would make me less than my best, and to say "Yes!" to the challenges and opportunities that will make me grow and improve my life.

...because total commitment is my constant companion, and personal integrity is my lifetime mentor.

...because I am learning to avoid the tempting shortcuts that can lead to disappointment, and the unhealthy habits that could result in defeat.

...because I have a well-earned confidence in myself, a high regard for my teammates and co-workers, and a healthy respect for those in authority over me.

...because I have learned to accept criticism, not as a threat, but as an opportunity to examine my attitudes and to improve my skills.

...because I persevere in the midst of obstacles and fight on in the face of defeat.

...because I am made in the image and likeness of my Creator, who gave me a burning desire, a measure of talent, and a strong faith to attempt the difficult and to overcome the seemingly impossible.

...because of my enthusiasm for life, my enjoyment of the present, and my trust in the future.

WILLIAM ARTHUR WARD

THOUGHTS OF A WINNER

Although I am only one out of a million, I am somebody, and that makes me as good as the next person.

There is nothing in this life I cannot do. There is no goal I cannot tackle and achieve success. If I feel deep down inside that something is important to me, then I can do it. If my mind can conceive it and believe it, then I know I can achieve it. Because self-pity is the seed of destruction, no longer will I drift through life feeling sorry for myself.

I will search for a goal, and with enough hard work, total commitment, determination, dedication, and self-sacrifice, I know I will reach it. I know there will be many times when it will seem that all the odds are against me, and I will have to fight one battle after another—*but I will not give up!*

AUTHOR UNKNOWN

Experience is the name we give to our mistakes.
By faith you can move mountains; but the important thing is,
not to move mountains, but to have faith.

A. BROCK

The noblest revenge is to forgive.

THOMAS FULLER

Recipe for having friends: be one.

We must not only give what we have; we must also give what we are.

It isn't your position that makes you happy or unhappy, it's your disposition.

There is no medicine like hope, no incentive so great, and no tonic so
powerful as expectation of something better tomorrow.

O. S. MARDEN

Kindness in words creates confidence.
Kindness in thinking creates profoundness. Kindness in giving creates love.

The distance on life's journey is marked not by the number of pages
torn from the calendar, but by the number of good deeds done.

We are shaped and fashioned by what we love.

GOETHE

The optimist recalls happy yesterdays, enjoys the hours of today,
and confidently expects that tomorrow will be a great day.

Instead of giving someone a piece of your mind,
give them a piece of your positive attitude.

He who lives without discipline is exposed to grievous ruin.

THOMAS KEMPIS

Winners believe they are winners because they've learned to act like winners—
right down to the smallest detail.

IT'S ALL UP TO YOU!

Your success depends upon you.
Your happiness depends on you.
You have to steer your own course.
You have to shape your own future.
You have to educate yourself.
You have to do your own thinking.
You have to live with your own conscience.
Your mind is yours and can be used only by you.
You come into this world alone.
You go to the grave alone.
You are alone with your inner thoughts during the journey through life.
You must make your own decisions.
You must abide by the consequences of your acts.
You alone can regulate your habits and make or unmake your health.
You alone can assimilate things mental and things material.
You have to do your own assimilation all through life.
You may be taught by a teacher, but you have to absorb the knowledge.
    She cannot implant it into your brain.
You alone can control your mind cells and your brain cells.
Before you is spread the wisdom of the ages, but unless you assimilate it,
    you derive no benefit from it; no one can force it into your cranium.
You alone can control your own muscles.
You must stand on your own feet, physically and metaphorically.
You must take your own steps.
You must take control of your mental and physical machinery, and make
    something of yourself.

You cannot have battles fought for you. You must fight them yourself.
You have to be the captain of your own destiny.
You have to master your own faculties.
You have to solve your own problems.
You have to form your own ideals.
You have to create your own ideas.
You must govern your own tongue.
Your real life is your own thoughts.
Your thoughts are of your own making.
Your character is your own handiwork.
 You alone can select the materials that go into it.
 You alone can reject what is not fit to go into it.
You are the creator of your own personality.
You can be disgraced by no person's hand but your own.
You have to write your own record.
You have to build your own monument—or dig your own pit.

Which are you doing?

THE BEGINNING

The German poet Goethe once stated, "The writer only begins a book. The reader finishes it." In other words, this book becomes a powerful tool as you add a personal dimension to it through applying these thoughts and ideas in a way that they may enrich your life. It is my hope that these insights that I have had the pleasure of sharing with you will spark a new enthusiasm in all that you do. Take stock in yourself and use your burning desire and determination to rise above the challenges and adversities that may confront you each day. You are the one responsible for making the changes necessary to improve the quality of your life. You are the most important ingredient to your success and happiness. You must not let go of the belief that everything you want from life is within your reach. Never, never give up pursuing that which will bring you happiness and fulfillment.

Once a student had decided to quit school, saying he was bored by his lessons. His teacher desperately tried to persuade him to stay with it. "Young man," the teacher said, "you can't quit. Throughout history there are examples of great leaders who are remembered because they didn't quit. Benjamin Franklin didn't quit. Thomas Edison didn't quit. Henry Ford didn't quit. And then there was Carl Johnson." "Who?" the student questioned. "Who in the world is Carl Johnson?" "See," the teacher replied, "You don't remember him because he quit!"

We are all students in life, learning and growing, trying to find peace of mind, happiness and success. Grenville Kleiser wrote: "Life is a great school in which you are constantly learning how to work, plan, and achieve. The schoolmaster of life may seem stern and relentless, but the discipline is for your ultimate good." Adversity, discouragement, failure, mistakes, and obstacles are nothing more than teachers of self-discovery. You can become all that you want and deserve to be. You can accomplish the extraordinary, but you must never quit pursuing your dreams and aspirations. The choice is yours to make. Philosopher and writer Henry David Thoreau wrote, "If one advances confidently in the direction of his dreams, and endeavors to live the life he has imagined, he will meet with a success unexpected in common hours."

To grow a tree, one must first start with a seed. Plant that seed and provide it with the proper nourishment so that it will grow into something great. Dreams are to people what seeds are to trees.

Every goal begins as a dream. Nourish your dreams, and let them grow and become the catalyst that motivates you to action. Remember, if you don't have dreams, your dreams can never come true.

I wish you the best of happiness, success, and personal achievement as you uncover and awaken the greatness that lies within you. Let today be a new start, a fresh beginning.

Carpe diem! (Seize the day!)

It is one of the most beautiful compensations of this life that no man can sincerely try to help another without helping himself.

RALPH WALDO EMERSON

Share the Pep of

THE PORTABLE PEP TALK

Motivational Morsels for Inspiring You to Succeed

A L E X A N D E R   L O C K H A R T

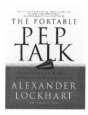

256 pages. Trade paperback. $12.95ea ISBN 09643035-7-4

Would you like additional copies of this book? Why not share the Pep in *The Portable Pep Talk* with a loved one, friend, or co-worker. Each copy, a tremendous value at only $12.95 (plus shipping), will enrich the lives of everyone who receives this valued treasure of inspiration.

Available at your favorite bookstore, or send check or money order to:

Zander Press
P.O. Box 11741
Richmond, VA. 23230

Please include $2.00 for postage and handling.
(Virginia residents must include appropriate sales tax)
Please allow 2 weeks for delivery
Or Call 1-800-450-7737

Also Available on Audio Cassette

The Portable Pep Talk: Motivational Morsels for Inspiring You to Succeed (Book-on-Tape)
A convenient way to listen to thought provoking and inspirational stories in the comfort of your home, automobile, and anyplace where you have access to a tape player. Order your tape today for only $15.95 each plus $2.00 shipping and handling.

POSITIVE CHARGES

544 Ways To Stay Upbeat During Downbeat Times

ALEXANDER LOCKHART

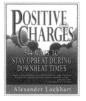

224 pages. Trade Paperback. $9.95ea ISBN 0-9643035-5-8

Your attitude and outlook toward your everyday experiences play an important role in getting the results you want in your life. Inside this bestselling book, you will find a diverse collection of inspiring statements and insightful principles that will cheer you up in dark moments and uplift your spirits.

Available at your favorite bookstore, or send check or money order to:

Zander Press
P.O. Box 11741
Richmond, VA. 23230

Please include $2.00 for postage and handling.

(Virginia residents must include appropriate sales tax)

Please allow 2 weeks for delivery

Or Call 1-800-450-7737

Also Available on Audio Cassette

Read by the Author

Positive Charges: 544 Ways To Stay Upbeat During Downbeat Times (Book-on-Tape)

by Alexander Lockhart

Includes music written and performed by the Author

90 min. audio. $12.95ea ISBN 0-9643035-9-0

JOIN THE PEP RALLY!

Perhaps you have a "motivational morsel" in the form of a story, personal experience, article, poem, or quotation that you would like to share with others and that you feel belongs in future *Pep Talk* volumes. Is there something that you read in a newspaper, magazine or newsletter that pepped up your spirits? If so, we would love to hear from you. You may send your favorites to:

Zander Press—Dept. 36
P.O. Box 11741
Richmond, VA. 23230
peptalk@zanderpress.com

Upon the publication and inclusion in future Pep Talk books, you and the author will be recognized for your submission. And to show our appreciation for taking time to share your "morsel" with us, we will send you a valuable coupon that can be used toward other Zander Press publications and audio programs. Thank you in advance for your contribution.

ABOUT THE AUTHOR

Alexander Lockhart is a nationally acclaimed author, inspirational speaker and corporate trainer in the areas of success psychology and personal development. He is founder of Positive Performance, a training and development company offering workshops throughout the country on personal motivation and peak performance skills.

America's top corporations have relied on his expertise to train their sales groups, support personnel and management to develop higher performance levels and effective bottom line results. Alexander uses simple strategies to reinforce his message in an innovative and enlightening presentation which reflects over twelve years of accumulated knowledge and hands-on experience in sales, management and marketing.

Having devoted over a decade studying the most practical and powerful methods of self-help psychology, Alexander is dedicated to sharing these effective insights to help others overcome obstacles and reach their personal best. He has written numerous articles on personal growth and is the author of the bestselling book, *Positive Charges: 544 Ways to Stay Upbeat During Downbeat Times.*

For more information on personal and professional coaching, workshops or to request a complete catalogue of audio/video presentations and other motivational products on personal and professional excellence contact:

Positive Performance
c/o Zander Press-Dept. 36
P.O. Box 11741
Richmond, VA. 23230
info@zanderpress.com

BIBLIOGRAPHY

And Suggested Reading

Allen, James. *As A Man Thinketh.* New York: Grosset and Dunlap, 1959.

Bland, Glen. *Success! The Glen Bland Method.* Wheaton: Tyndale House, 1972.

Brown, Les. *Live Your Dreams.* New York: William Morrow, 1992.

Carnegie, Dale. *How To Stop Worrying And Start Living.* New York: Simon and Schuster, 1984.
---. *How To Win Friends And Influence People.* New York: Simon and Schuster, 1981.

Carroll, Lewis. *Alice In Wonderland.* New York: Grosset and Dunlap, 1946.

Collier, Robert. *The Secret Of The Ages.* Tarrytown: Robert Collier Publications, 1948.

Conwell, Russell H. *Acres Of Diamonds.* Uhrichville: Barbour and Company, 1993.

Giblin, Les. *How To Have Power And Confidence In Dealing With People.* Englewood Cliffs: Prentice-Hall, 1956.

Hay, Gilbert. *Golden Harvest.* New York: Doubleday and Company Inc., 1979.

Guest, Edgar. *The Path To Home.* New York: The Reily and Lee Co., 1953. ---. *The Collected Verse Of Edgar Guest.* New York: The Reily and Lee Co., 1934.

Hill, Napoleon. *Think And Grow Rich.* New York: Ballantine Books, 1937.

Kleiser, Grenville. *The Bridge You'll Never Cross and Other Poems.* New York: Funk and Wagnells Company, 1948.

Kohe, Martin J. *Your Greatest Power.* Chicago: Success Unlimited Inc., 1953.

Maltz, Dr. Maxwell. *Psycho-Cybernetics.* New York: Pocket Books, 1960.

Mandino, Og. *The Greatest Miracle In The World.* New York: Bantam, 1975. ---. *The Greatest Secret In The World.* New York: Bantam, 1978.

Schwartz, Dr. David J. *The Magic Of Thinking Big.* New York: Simon and Schuster, 1987.

Stone, W. Clement. *The Success System That Never Fails.* Englewood Cliffs: Prentice-Hall, 1962.

Waitly, Denis. *The Psychology Of Winning.* Chicago: Nightingale-Conant, 1984.

Ziglar, Zig. *See You At The Top.* Grenta: Pelican Publishing, 1975.